Radhouan Ben Amar

The Fragmentation of the Pr
and The Crisis of De

Radhouan Ben Amara

The Fragmentation of the Proper Name and The Crisis of Degree

Deconstructing *King Lear*

LIT

Bibliographic information published by Die Deutsche Bibliothek
Die Deutsche Bibliothek lists this publication in the Deutsche
Nationalbibliografie; detailed bibliographic data are available in the
Internet at http://dnb.ddb.de.

ISBN 3-8258-6736-6

© LIT VERLAG Münster   2004
Grevener Str./Fresnostr. 2   48159 Münster
Tel. 0251-23 50 91   Fax 0251-23 19 72
e-Mail: lit@lit-verlag.de   http://www.lit-verlag.de

Distributed in North America by:

Transaction Publishers
New Brunswick (U.S.A.) and London (U.K.)

Transaction Publishers   Tel.: (732) 445 - 2280
Rutgers University   Fax: (732) 445 - 3138
35 Berrue Circle   for orders (U. S. only):
Piscataway, NJ 08854   toll free (888) 999 - 6778

In memory of my generous mother Halima.

CONTENTS

i

ACKNOWLEDGEMENTS

This book is the result of a long process of reflection on Shakespeare's work in general, and *King Lear* in particular. During the years when the contents of this book were taking shape, numerous friends and colleagues gave me benefit of their interest. Others provided me with occasion to discuss my ideas in public. I owe a particular debt of gratitude to my Rabbit, especially for her patience and valuable advice. I am grateful to the following for their encouragements, suggestions and help: Dario Calimani, always sharp and mild, rough and fine, strange and familiar. Cristina Giorcelli, an active refined observer who has always encouraged new born babies in old folks' homes; and Giulia Fabi, keen symbol of measure and straightforwardness. Maria Diedrich was generous with her time, advice and friendship, very supportive, always the line and the *don*.

Thanks are also due to Karen Heller and Sarah Alexander, who patiently read the manuscript, making suggestions that substantially improved the book; Maria Antonietta Santoro who meticulously took care of the formatting and the reading. Several colleagues and friends assisted me with suggestions, encouragements, and criticisms.

I want here to acknowledge the pioneering oeuvre of Jacques Derrida which provided me with a critical terrain and an intellectual project. The works of Jean-Pierre Richard, Maurice Blanchot, Merleau-Ponty, Nietzsche, Heidegger, Michel Foucault, Paul Ricoeur, and Edward Said have been formative in my thinking as a whole. Many of my ideas on the Body, the Estrangement, and the Other have sparked off by the novels of North African and Afro American writers.

My children Layli and Tahar have been true companions: their interruptions, their encouraging "bruhaha" have been frequent and irreplaceable.

I thank the Reader to bear with me the incompletion that accompanies the act of writing; I never ventured to make any forcible entrance; I got wounded many times while writing.

WHY PREFACE?

Introductions or prefaces are frequently the occasion for a writer to question the function of a book's beginning. I must frankly say that I have nothing to question or to answer. Nothing to propose either. Nietzsche said in his preface to the second edition of *The Gay Science* that if the reader has not lived through experiences similar to those of the book, the preface probably will not greatly help. So I prefer to overturn the traditional function of introductions, to resist summary language and the expectation of summarisable conclusions. The dual tyranny of age and our uncertain era make me refuse introductions and conclusions, for I see them as mere consolations. Michel Foucault, on the other hand, liked introductions and used them "to set a mood or to set the record straight about this or that; they were for him, as a matter of fact, occasions to play seriously."

Translators, as we all know, have less trouble with introductions because the function of translating encourages talk and commentary about what goes on in the text. I am not translating anything here, and so I would prefer to let the language go on outside the purview of commentary and comments. No introduction and consequently no conclusion. The use of summarising, forced introductions, or reporting conclusions can be a great problem for those who do not like to confine the meaning to a one-way destination. How can we free ourselves from the image of a completed textual corpus that once completed, could be well introduced and summarised as though it were finished once and for all? I think that introductions and conclusions usurp, violate and assault the free ongoing and open development of discourses, as well as the polyvalence or multiplicity of meanings contained in language. They hurt the comprehensible finality of language, its dimensions, its possibilities, and its lack of meaning. How would we introduce, for example, the contradictory meanings of a word? How to introduce what we are going to talk about before explaining it? Of course, that introduce, might be played in its senses of to make known, to insert, to inscribe, to open. But how might an opening to the text as text, make itself known? We are not supposed to make the history of the text dealt with, before reading the text itself. An introduction in this way would be a prejudice to the contents of the text to be studied. We do not need any primary seeing. Introductions, to tell the truth, pick up ideas and themes that are yet to come. What is not yet said is always more important than what is announced or said beforehand. What is most important remains so far unsaid: there are few things we know too well; now we have to learn how to forget well, and "to be good at not knowing, as artists." A boundary – says Heidegger – "is not that at which something stops but, as the Greeks recognized, the boundary is that from which something begins its presencing."

NOTE ON THE TEXT

All references to *King Lear* are to the Arden edition of the play, edited by Kenneth Muir (London and New York: Routledge, 1975).

References to Shakespeare's other tragedies are to The Peebles Classic Library, edited by Sandy Lesberg (New York: Peebles Press International Inc).

PART ONE
THE CRACK'D BOND: THE NAME AND THE
ESTRANGED BODY

What's in a name? That which we call a rose
By any other name would smell as sweet.
Shakespeare

Soul is only a word for something about the body.
Nietzsche

The place where they lay, it has a name – it has none. They did not lie there.
Celan

I write in order to lose my name.
Bataille

There is no intention behind the title of this book to proceed with a literary approach. I am instead offering a theoretical practice for reading *King Lear* in a different way. My fundamental aim is that of reading more than interpreting. *King Lear* is for me only a text, a writing; and writing calls for reading. Writing could be then situated as the by product that happens between the act of production and what is produced. What interests me most is this space, in which this play is communicated, disseminated, displayed, incorporated, limited, put into text, and differentiated. My approach is unlimited, meant to open up other worlds and other spaces. Not one choice, but many choices and many paths. *King Lear* inscribes not one path or the other, but the intersection, the meeting place, the seam, and above all the trace. Should I admit that I have been pondering the meaning of this play for a long time; it is not singular, it does not lie in positive or negative terms; but rather, is inextricably resident in the tensions between terms, and also between competing cultural forces, in every side's definition of the term, which itself is utterly inscribed in the other side's definition. My reading of the play is in this case oriented towards an understanding of meaning as event, rather than structure. In this tension, meaning is elusive, mobile, inevitably non-local. What becomes urgently important in the study of the tragedy of *King Lear* is to explore the rich semiotic associations of those mythologies of origin and closure, rampant throughout the play, and to build up a movement that is not based on the opposition of presence and absence, but rather on the systematic play of differences, or traces of differences, by which, elements relate to one another. A delicate and most difficult enterprise, that of fragmentation and dislocation. Writes Derrida:

knows of no proper itinerary which would lead from its beginning to its end and back again, nor does its movements admit of a centre. Because it is structurally liberated from any living meaning, it is always possible that it means nothing at all or that it has no decidable meaning. There is no end to its parodying with meaning, grafted here and there, beyond any contextual body or finite code. [...] Its secret is rather the possibility that indeed it might have no secret, that it might only be pretending to be simulating some hidden truth within its folds. Its limit is not only stipulated by its structure but is in fact intimately con-fused with it. (1)

Fragmentation is both a limit and an ineluctable transgression of the limit. It is to be found in the gulf between the text of the play as other, and the decoder of the text; and again within the tensions and textures of difference in the heap of fragmentations themselves. In the case of *King Lear*, these tensions are generated by sons/daughters and parents, political decisions, reason and madness, monologues and dialogues, waste, friendship, and many others:

GLOUCESTER: These eclipses in the sun and moon portend no good to us: though the wisdom of Nature can reason it thus and thus, yet Nature finds itself scourg'd by the sequent effects. Love cools, friendship falls off, brothers divide; in cities, mutinies; in countries, discord; in palaces, treason; and the bond crack'd 'twixt son and father. This villain of mine comes under the prediction; there's son against father: the king falls from bias of nature; there's father against child. We have seen the best of our time: machinations, hollowness, treachery, and all ruinous disorders follow us disquietely to our graves. (I, ii, 100–111)

Apart from what they apparently mean, Gloucester's words represent what René Girard calls the "crisis of degree" of the whole play, and it is here well condensed with all its ingredients. These lines suggest what will happen in the play both as event and as structure: social fissure and psychic fragmentation. They also foresee the great eclipse of sovereignty in the play, and demonstrate Shakespearean culture not as some self enclosed sign system of endlessly circling representations, but as the threshold of a vital ongoing process based on discontinuity. Writes René Girard, commenting Gloucester's words: "Chacun, comme toujours, dit la vérité de l'autre, celle d'un désir mimétique, bien sûr, sans voir la vérité de son propre désir qui est au fond le même et, par conséquent, source à la fois de lucidité et d'aveuglement chez la plupart des hommes. [. . .] Ce que Shakespeare entend discréditer, ce sont les explications de type magique et non la crise elle-même; il croit manifestement à la réalité de cette dernière et fait de l'effacement des différences dans l'ensemble des rapports humains la substance même de ses meilleures pièces." (Girard 224 – 225)

The 'crisis of degree' as understood by René Girard is therefore the crisis of hierarchy, the crisis of difference and differential order. Degree, from the Latin "gradus", designates the step of a staircase, or the rung of a ladder, and consequently a level difference ("a level to all high designs"). In a wider sense, this word could also mean distinction, discrimination, hierarchy, difference. Degree is also that eternal gap between justice and injustice, the spacing out, that must exist between "al halal" and "al haram", as the Arab Muslims would say, that is, the allowed and the prohibited, in order to prevent them from being confused. Justice here is to be understood neither as something pure, nor as an exercise of pure impartiality, a quest for a perfect equilibrium, but simply as an imbalance, with a fixed modality, just like all that is cultural. Justice, if such thing exists, has to do with these little bits and fragments; it has to do with the remains, the rags and rogues, the nobodies. Shakespeare seems to suggest that in a given culture, all singular differences, all particular levels or gradations have something in common, a certain kinship: all, in their differences and diversities fall within the province of a unique and same principle, a differential order, on which the stability and the existence of cultural systems stand and resist.

In *King Lear*, the main cause of this crisis of degree is that catastrophic and disastrous passage from the external mediation to the internal mediation, or mediate inference: Lear who invites his three daughters to show the love they bear him. Instead of preventing a certain mimetic competition between his daughters, he does but provoke it, proposing himself as a competitive object of desire. We must acknowledge on this level that desire in this play is not only shown through the words which represent it, or recount it, but it is represented by words sufficiently characterised, sufficiently brilliant, triumphant, to make themselves loved, in a very fetishist way. Lear's search for a lost object can be seen as a secure investment of energy as long as one can determine that the object will remain lost. If reading allows, we could say that Lear is haunted by the fear of becoming a woman, of losing, together with authority, his manhood, his virility, and of being reduced to a child. It is the Fool (pointing to Lear) who focuses on the looseness of the King's virility: "That's a sheal'd peascod" (I, iv, 197). Peascod is a metaphor that demonstrates that Lear's movements are inscribed within what in Freudian terms could be called a "radical dimension of castration." Lear will then examine himself together with his madness under a feminised title:

> That thou hast power to shake my manhood thus,
> That these hot tears, which break from me perforce,
> Should make thee worth them. Blasts and fogs upon
> thee! (I, iv, 295 – 297)

> And let not women's weapons, water-drops
> Stain my man's cheeks! ... (II, iv, 275 – 276)

The magnitude of Lear's sorrow is too great for him to bear. He cannot sustain this enormous weight of sorrow, and support these heavy draperies of grief. Unmanned by his grief, Lear is feminised by his tears and excluded from being an acknowledged mourner by his gender. His feminisation is a measure of his mental disorder. Any sign of emotion such as tears is to be interpreted as pathological. Anxieties about masculinity are commonly diagnosed features of shell shock victims: loss of memory, loss of sight, dementia. Grief, in Freudian terms works also as a freeing of the libido from the lost love object. There is here a whole confusion of gender roles, social positions, and psychological states. We can even say that unconsciously,

Lear wants to be the son of his daughters; he wants to be reborn and penetrate into the bellies of his daughters. It is the Fool who says it clearly: "Thou mad'st thy daughters thy mothers." The belly becomes the object upon which Lear holds his desire of penetration. Nature itself becomes a belly, a grave. Need without desire is blind; it has no object, it is identical to itself, closed within itself, tautological and autistic. This may explain the fact that Lear, through this desire, links the need to an object, – be it the belly or the grave – in order to submit it to a certain fixed order. One aspect of his madness is the ensemble of these successive exclusions of the bellies he wanted to penetrate. When Lear sought refuge in nature (storm), he took it for a belly, an image which would substitute the other bellies he was excluded from: "Rumble thy belly ful! Spite, fire, spout, rain!// Nor rain, wind, thunder, fire, are my daughters." (III, ii, 14 – 15)

The storm is the grave, the object of the fixated desire. Lear values the grave and takes it for a belly; but here again he is excluded:

> You do me wrong to take me out o'th' grave;
> Thou art a soul in bliss; but I am bound
> Upon a wheel of fire ... That mine own tears
> Do scold like molten lead. (IV, vii, 45 – 48)

These lines are a disguised and symptomatic recognition of what incites Lear to yearn for the grave. The grave represents the indignation at human failing and nature's complicity in our mortality. It emphasises our inevitable immersion in death. It negates energy, integrity and creativity. It suggests that human observation is never definitive, that our knowledge is temporary and incomplete. Meditation on the grave becomes meditation on the limits of human power and human language; the limits of our will. Although there is a speaking presence called Lear, all seems very offensive and offending to his presence. Thus, this delight in chaos, danger and multiplicity that abounds in the whole play. It may be said that Lear's yearning for the grave is visionary knowledge, attained through a dissolution of boundaries between self and other, self and nature, that enables a larger, more dynamic, more empowering knowledge of self and other:

> Thou wert better in a grave than answer with

thy uncover'd body this extremity of the skies. Is
man no more than this? (III, iv, 99 – 101)

Maybe the grave is not a place, but a fact, or a mystery that is never
fixed! In this way, the grave becomes a fine and a private space of privilege,
especially for that property owning elite. This reading cannot certainly exclude another reading: desire does not necessarily have an essential relation
to lack. Desire can be also an affirmation, and consequently mourning itself an affirmation as well. Frustrated, bereft, Lear is bound upon a wheel
of fire that leads him to the real grave. It is on this level that we may speak
about the close relationship between death and desire (love). Love unfulfilled leads to death. Writes Mayoux: "La mort y est melée comme une
donnée qu'il faut accepter. L'amour joue avec elle, défie la mort, forme et
triomphe de la haine. L'amour prend la mort comme déguisement, mais il
trouve la mort par malentendu. C'est l'apothéose de l'amour, l'apothéose
d'un érotique du langage, où l'amour se fond aussi exquisiment dans la
mort plus tard chez Keats." (2)

Death, for certain, is the implacable enemy of human desire. As W.B.
Yeats puts it: "Man is in love and loves what vanishes,/ What more is there
to say?" Well a great deal more actually, including most philosophy and
art, neither of which would exist as we know them but for death being
intolerable. And even more so is religion. The wonderfully perverse thing
about Christianity – as Jonathan Dollimore says – is not that it invented
God and eternal life to lessen the trauma of death, but that it intensified
the trauma by making Man responsible for death: original sin, that sublime
mythical blend of abjection and hubris, brought sex and death into the world
and made them inseparable. Surely this is one reason for the even more
shocking fact that death has not only been dreaded; it has also been longed
for, desired. Hamlet, in the world's most famous theatrical meditation on
death, tells us that to die is "a consummation// Devoutly to be wished."
Death, the enemy of human desire, is also what it yearns for, and identifies
with. Though this paradox is always haunting literature and philosophy, and
often emerges as its obsessive focus, most modern professionals in these
fields seem to find the paradox too disturbing to confront. Maybe tragic
death could be imagined as a release from the frustrations of human desire,
and human mortality.

There is in Shakespeare a delight in the juxtaposition of contrasting tones: the tragic and the grotesque, the comic and the pathetic, the cynical and the magnanimous; a strong interest in human psychology, particularly the psychology of desire in its many varieties: verbal fertility, linguistic play, discursive gaming. Variety and flexibility are Shakespeare's essential habits of mind and forms of expression. Desire becomes a sort of bewilderment, because one can never be sure whether one is running towards what one desires or running away from it; and when you think you have seen what you most desire, it destroys you. When desire is no more inscribed within the time and the space of a corpus of words, man loses his centre: he implodes; life loses its weight. This is what really happened to Lear. There is a whole revealing sexuality concealed in Lear's exercise of language: concealed, maybe because it is difficult to figure out, to project or to say a desire. Is it representable to desire and to speak at the same time? Lear transforms in this way his unnameable desire into a sort of obligation for his daughters, and the ceremony (sharing the kingdom) that he organises for this event, cannot but coincide with his abdication. Behaving thus, Lear tenders his resignation not only as a king, but also as a father. The haste with which Goneril and Regan enter this game condemns them to the same destiny as their father. Consequently, a whole process of competition is triggered, and everything in the play becomes rivalry; even the choice of Edmund as a lover for both Goneril and Regan. This war between the two sisters prepares the various means and ways of destruction. What they all crave for is royal power – a power that their violence destroys as it contaminates the whole kingdom. In the whole kingdom, however, the transvalutation of all values makes that knaves like Edmund are socially promoted, instead of the innocent brothers. This way, we are led to the real meaning of degree. Shakespeare himself uses that very word in *Troilus and Cressida*:

> ULYSSES: What honey is expected? Degree being vizarded,
> The unworthiest shows as fairly in the mask.
> The heavens themselves, the planets, and this centre
> Observe degree, priority, and place,
> Insisture, course, proportion, season, form,
> Office, and custom, in all line of order [...].
> When degree is

shak'd,
Which is the ladder to all high designs,
The enterprise is sick. How could communities,
Degrees in schools, and brotherhoods in cities,
Peaceful commerce from dividable shores,
The primogenitive and due of birth,
Prerogative of age, crowns, sceptres, laurels,
But by degree, stand in authentic place?
Take but degree away, untune that string,
And, hark! What discord follows; each thing
meets
In mere oppugnancy: the bounded waters
Should lift their bosoms higher than the shores,
And make a sop of all this solid globe:
Strength should be lord of imbecility,
And the rude son should strike his father dead. (I, iii, 83 – 88/
    101 – 113)

It is above all inside Lear's family that this principle becomes apparent.
Cordelia dies unjustly because she refuses to bite into the mimetic bait; her
sisters die justly because they bit into it. The crisis of degree includes everybody, with no exception. This leads us to conclude that the transgression
in this play is therefore an act outside the pre-established realm of law. Law
is here an element of calculation, which would appear to be just. But justice
is incalculable; it demands that we calculate the incalculable. Justice is thus
an experience of the impossible. Law is not justice. King Lear's first act of
transgression is his decision to divide the kingdom between his daughters,
as he, in his old age "crawls to death":

LEAR: Meanwhile, we shall express our dark purpose.
Give me the map there. Know that we have divided
In three our kingdom; and 'tis our fast intent
To shake all cares and business from our age,
Conferring them on younger strengths, while we
Unburden'd crawl toward death. (I, i, 35 – 40)

Words of this type situate perhaps better than others, the place where discourse can no longer dominate, judge, or decide. They dictate in a certain way the laws of receivability. There looms an adventure of power and unpower, a play of potency and impotence, a size of desire very impressive, out of all proportion to any type of discourse. At first reading, "dark purpose" could mean a secret intention, that is to say, to give the best share to the daughter who loves Lear most, and who Lear assumes is Cordelia. Another reading directs us to the idea of renunciation. In other words, Lear's "dark purpose" exposes a world that is to be destroyed. It involves nothing less than division, the drawing of boundaries, the parcelling up of his own country. And at the same time, when Lear calls for the map, the play begins to deal with issues of much larger concern. It changes its focus from personality to politics, and a whole way of life. As a matter of fact, Lear's project reduces his spiritual, unifying kingship into a real estate deal. This "We have divided in three our kingdom" reduces a political and emotional unity to disconnected fractions of the whole; even the sentence structure itself is fractured. From the first moments of the play, a wholly debased kind of loving can be seen to operate throughout Lear's court and to inform all of its procedures. This connection with calculation, measurement and money receives direct confirmation in Gloucester's words: "It did always seem so to us; but now, in the division of the kingdom, it appears not which of the Dukes he values most; for equalities are so weigh'd that curiosity in neither can make choice of either's moiety." (I, i, 3 – 7)

The terms *division, values, equalities, weigh'd, choice, moiety,* tell us a great deal about a kingdom that is about to be fragmented, portioned, shared out and parcelled up. They also reveal that spirit of loving in which the sharing is to take place. This also shows clearly the real narrative of the play: the story of Lear and the story of Gloucester. If Lear – as many critics have argued – reduces love to the level of the assessment of land and property values, Gloucester reduces it to the level of lust gratified by a whore. In both cases, money corrupts love and affection. The map itself is nothing but a symbol for that process of diminution. Mapping of this kind is nothing but a culpable violation of Nature and it should stand as a crime. It is a lie because the map has been brought about in the name of love. The destruction of love is a consequence of the destruction of the map. But in any case, we begin here with an awareness of something missing or not visible, of an incompleteness in the description of the situation through the expression "dark purpose."

We should think that the engine which drives the first section of the play is the desire to inspect and understand this present-absence contained in the expression "dark purpose." Why does a reasonable person seek a gloomy objective? Are objectives or aims supposed to be dark? Maybe this is an image or a metaphor invested with some sense of phenomenological presence, used in a disjunctive meaning that does not highlight any communicable intellectual or emotional message. We know the importance of metaphor in Shakespeare's dramatic poetry. He excels in mingling analogy and metaphor as the most acute representations of a mind engaged in thought. He uses them to represent the turbulence of his characters' minds. Though aware of the risk of metaphor as notoriously open to failure, Shakespeare chooses to run that risk throughout his work. "Dark purpose" translates in this vein the present absence into alienation from self and others. This expression already exceeds Lear's knowledge, and is an anticipation — conscious or unconscious — of his gloomy, soon to be-lived experiences. Lear anticipates the realisation of his fears, and therefore the potential loss of insight. The value of this concealment of the true meaning of "dark purpose" lies in its inclusion of the diversity and decenteredness of King Lear himself, and is meant as a protection against the codification of a single perspective. One way to understand this unclear meaning is that it represents the local illocality of the present, be it of Lear or of his entourage. It consequently measures not the absence of a past that must be supplemented, but a past so supplemented that it has overtaken its own future. It is a past which pronounces itself everywhere. The surplus of this illocality is both everywhere and nowhere; it is the pronouncement emerging from an array of fragments and from the ruptures transforming them. "Dark purpose" can also be seen as a frozen emphasis on a thing that is out of sight, an allusion to a decision, or something made, that will probably remain hidden. It is the present misinformed, or the present groping after what is only remembered of the past, and which implies its movement into the future. It is the rupture of the present that is not aware of the present past, thinking it is the continuation into the future, without foreseeing the future. In other words, Lear's misperception of the present, which is based on the past, informs his future, which will be misunderstood. The paradox is that for Lear, only the "now," the "meanwhile" matters. There is no more time for Lear's past in the present; or rather there are no more lines in the time of "ripeness" that is past. His actions can no longer be made to have a permanent effect. Lear does not realise that in sharing the kingdom, he has already made a serious political decision, and hence, he provoked a quid-pro quo within himself. Misunderstanding is not only between the King and his daughters, but within Lear himself: it is the true expression of a discrepancy and an inadequacy between what Lear does (sharing the king-dom) and what Lear wants (possessing his daughters affectively). Goneril and Regan's ingratitude would not have led Lear to wretchedness, had he left something for himself; this is what Lear himself confesses: "What! Has his daughters brought him// to this pass?// Couldst thou save nothing? Didst thou give// them all?" (III, iv, 62 – 64)

Apropos of this "I" who speak(s) in the third person singular, it is ob-vious that a disproportionate detachment at the heart of the sentences that Lear pronounces makes him as remote as the third person "he." Sentences become confused in the distance, where self erasure brings out this third person, who has been speaking at all times, and who always remains the same. This is because death has already exercised its sovereignty. Lear's grammatical renunciation is a self negation. In other terms, we are dealing in fact with a substitutive relationship in which the place of a self is usurped by another self. This is the result of a plain and simple fact: the speaking subject is also the subject about which it speaks. It is in a way speech about speech that will lead us to an outside in which the speaking subject Lear disappears.

Deciding to divide the kingdom, Lear renounces himself and his power of decision. But the paradox is that he renounces his throne, expecting oth-ers to continue treating him as a king. An analysis of the first scene in Act One, shows this split within Lear himself, a wavering between two identi-ties: that of Lear, invested with royal power, firmness, and a certain prestige: "We have divided in three our kingdom"; the other identity is that he is the representative of this authority, only in principle. Lear has dissolved his au-thority, and even the use of "We" becomes ridiculous. The serious tone of the king becomes comical, and the grandeur involved in the plural pronoun "We" becomes rather the paradoxical expression of a real petty weakness. This wavering between greatness and pettiness, could also be perceived on the level of confusion in the pronouns he uses to speak of himself. In the same declamatory speech, when addressing his daughters, Lear uses at the same time the pronouns "I" and "We": "I do invest you jointly with my power//

Only we shall retain.[...]//The name and all th'addition to a king." (I, i, 129 – 135)

Behaving or misbehaving this way, Lear deprives himself of the value or the meaning of the trace. This deprivation and its resultant mortal danger produces the eruption of his madness, which means in real terms, the eruption of the mind's lack of discipline. Discipline, in Foucauldian terms means on the one hand a certain knowledge, and on the other, correction and control. Knowledge supposes therefore control and self containment. Lear should be disciplined, that is to say, punished. But on the other hand, this lack of discipline needs to be defended, and not only eradicated or suppressed. It is not chaos, but an uninterrupted, well mannered war within Lear and within Shakespeare's writing, in which poetry becomes the art of making and unmaking, the relationship to an impossible presence, the irreversible usage of energy. It is as if poetry were a way of cheating death.

This is in brief what is meant by fragment thinking. It is that "crack in the bond," an irreparable loss of presence which reveals madness as the centre of every human exchange. In this play, the proper name Lear is disfigured, disrupted, displaced from the beginning, and sends us back to its first letters: Real. The truth of Lear is that he is a shadow, an appearance, an unreality without any consistency, without any contents, without any being. The shadow evidently belongs to the world outside, with its mindless energies. It is that thinning out phase which is another name for dying. Its effect is to erase and blot out every lingering impression of reflection that has come before. Lear has no reality, he is not real, or rather, he is Lear, the caricature of real, the inversion of it. In other words, Lear is the unreality of sense, just as he is the sense of unreality:

Who is that can tell me who I am? [...]
FOOL: Now thou art an O without
a figure. I am better than thou art; I am a
fool, thou art nothing. (I, iv, 188 – 191)

Already in these words the problem of identity appears fully fledged. The problem of being comes up right at the beginning of the play when Lear starts questioning his very self, after realising that everything that distinguishes him — his title, his social position and his name — is lost. There is a quick shift from Lear's authority to Lear's alienation. The language of power has passed in a twinkle of an eye from his hands to his two daughters. On this level, it is the name of Lear that seems to be questioned; his name, once synonymous with authority, begins to fall apart, and crumble through repetition. When reality is threatened, the name is threatened too. The name Lear does not apply to him anymore, and we cannot even *lire* (read) his name now; it has become something like earl, no longer real, only lear: the name is destroyed by the distortion of its own words. The King becomes hence isolated, alienated, and reduced to "a dog obeyed in his office." Lear's being is carried away by the disintegration of his own name: between his heart and his name, there is no difference. We cannot say that Lear is disseminating or playing with his name; but we can agree that he feels an apparent desire to lose his name by disarticulating it. By losing his name, Lear makes it more and more intrusive; it occupies the whole field of sight, and as a result, gains in a certain way more and more ground. The more he loses his name, the more he gains by conceiving his proper name as a common noun. As his name indicates, Lear clearly shows that nothing is absolutely assured, neither kingship nor kinship. Lear gives and carries death, makes decisions on death, suspends it, stops it, then longs desperately for it. As a name, Lear can only inherit, and this is why the name is always and a priori a dead man's name, a name of death. What returns to the name never returns to the living; nothing ever comes back to the living. And if ever life returns, "it will return to the name but not to the living, in the name of the living as a name of the dead."(Derrida, *The Ear* 9) It is then by doing violence to himself that Lear promises to honour a pledge in the name of the name, in his name and in the name of the other(s). This is Lear's real "dark purpose": death. Maurice Blanchot would call this "le pas au-delà," the step beyond: approaching death in a step by step procedure of overstepping or of impossible transgression. The name of Lear becomes here a monument. He creates a way of seizing the language, putting it to his own use and installing its law. Lear, may we say, signifies upon language: he loses his name by winning it, and he wins it by losing it. As regards to this, we should notice that the word Lear does not seem a part of the game, because it is being held in reserve to designate the play in its entirety.

I cannot refrain from decoding this word as it applies to the title of the play. It is this meaning that I believe can be read in the word "Lear." It is the letter, the written letter, "lire, la *lettre*" tout court. Obviously, this is only a hypothesis, not that this reading of it is subjective; it is there in the autonomous meaning of the word. Lear's name is lost in a labyrinth which is the labyrinth of the ear, and we are summoned to proceed by seeking out all the edges, the inner walls, the passages, and the limits. Perhaps Shakespeare did not foresee it. He knew however, that language can never be disposed of absolutely, and that it is irremediably equivocal, open to two or more possibilities, always hiding something in the process of revealing everything, or nothing at all. And if, for example, Lacan seems to have had a fortress mentality about the effects of living in language, which Nietzsche once called a "prison-house," the American philosopher Stanley Cavell, on the contrary, conceives another construction, in an occasion of writing about Shakespeare, to respond to this question of the inevitable otherness of language in terms that do not imply alienation, incarceration, or abysmal lack:

Certainly we must not deny it: A word's reach exceeds its speaker's grasp, or what's a language for? This is to say: words recur, in unforetellable contexts; there would be no words otherwise; and no intentions otherwise, none beyond the, let me say, natural expressions of instinct; nor would there be the expression of desire, or ambition, or the making of a promise, or the acceptance of a prophecy. Unpredictable recurrence is not a sign of language's ambiguity but is a fact of language as such, that there are words. (Cavell: 12)

Countless instances in *King Lear* bear out the supremacy – for Shakespeare – of words over reason and probability. His passion for words was erudite as well as uncontrollable. Their meanings are often multiple and unfixed and their power is evident. In this respect, the play of language is Skakespeare's killing arm. This play occurs when a phrase refers not only to localised puns and wordplay, but also to an entire circulation of linguistic meaning, within and beyond the drama, which subsumes characters or in which characters participate but do not have any control. Beyond character and action, there is another site of the play, the play of language, where words refer to other significances. The term "play" is both literary and mimetic, both verb and noun, with several senses — game, gaming, exercise, free movement, amusement, pleasure, recreation, sport, trick, and in the times of Shakespeare it meant also "to boil." Hamlet, for instance, uses the word when he rebukes Rosencrantz and Guildenstern for trying to play him like an instrument (III, ii, 350 – 72). The term has a lot of play, in the sense of loose, unstable motion within a tolerable range, like the play of an automobile steering wheel.

"Free-play" reminds us also of the post structuralist theories of signifiers in language, and of the developmental theories of psychoanalysts such as Freud and Lacan, the aesthetic theories of rhetoricians, and the social theories of historians. For Derrida, for example, "play" is not fixed in finite discourse or structural symmetry or subjective intent: it happens, irresistibly, as a movement elsewhere of the traces of writing in the world. As a matter of fact, the concept of "jeu", to which Derrida refers frequently in his texts, is an interesting and important one, since it makes possible the paradox of a system being both finite and infinite, (de)limited and exceeded. Play is not therefore simply confined to isolated puns or homonyms, but can be a highly organised system of associations, wherein the effect of words is constantly felt. This happens a lot in the tragedy of *King Lear*, and examples are very numerous in this regard. It is these poetic playful expressions that are the condition of the opening of system, of its existence and persistence. Wordplay calls into mind Roland Barthes, who radically and nostalgically claimed that "the writer is someone who plays with the mother's body." (3)

King Lear is also a play(ing) about writing and reading. This spectre of "how to read" sends us back to the problem of interpretation, and deciphering. To write so as to possess meaning not only in the present but for all time: the hermeneutics of a will provide a fine instance – Derrida has observed – of the metaphysics of presence and mystique of speech. The first reference concerning reading and writing in *King Lear* is the letter coined by Edmund to fool Gloucester, apart from many other references connected to reading and deciphering:

> LEAR: Read thou this challenge; mark but the penning of it.
> GLOUCESTER: Were all thy letters suns, I could not see.
> EDGAR: [Aside.] I would not take this from report; it is,
> And my hearts breaks at it.
> LEAR: Read.

GLOUCESTER: What! with the case of eyes? (IV, vi, 135 –
142)

Reading seems divergent rather than convergent, moving rather than
fixed, always opening onto new grounds, always calling for interpretation
to be opened up anew. And in this fuzzy logic of the brain, meaning is inherently unstable. We can perhaps assume that the conflict of interpretation is a
deficit of interpretation itself, part of the logical weakness of hermeneutics.
This prompts the desire to get beyond interpretation to the meaning itself.
At this point, we could say that *King Lear* "does not talk to us; we interro-
gate it." Language endlessly spreads forth, while the subject "I" fragments,
disperses, scatters, disappearing into that naked space. Looked at from this
perspective, what seems to matter to Lear is that his property be distributed,
rather than consolidated. The division of Lear's kingdom provides, as a matter of fact, a frame for his dispersal of monological truth. Everything once
proper to King Lear is diffracted, and the scene of sharing the kingdom is
a metonymy for the diaspora of language and intertextuality of writing as it
circulates among those who compose the kingdom. Meaning itself eludes
expression and presence is for ever delayed with supplementary writing:

Lear: No rescue? What! a prisoner? I am even
The natural fool of Fortune. Use me well;
You shall have ransom. Let me have surgeons;
I am cut to th'brains. (IV, vi, 188 – 191)

Meaning is here plunged into a polysemous riot at the point where text
and body fuse, discourse and power are one. Writing becomes an orphan
language at its most carnivalesque and delinquent state. If the only site for
language is indeed this solitary sovereignty of the speaking "I", then in principle nothing can limit it: not the one to whom it is addressed, not the truth
of what it says, not the values or systems of representation it utilises. It is
no longer a discourse or a communication of meaning here, but a spreading
forth of language in its raw state, an unfolding of pure exteriority. Hence,
King Lear's truth is somehow a by product of a series of inherent tensions
between forces, and therefore his character's self is both created and transformed by the very process of verbal articulation. His being is invented

rhetorically, and this verbal rhetoric is of course accompanied by a visual rhetoric of stage gestures and actions. We believe that Lear will be inscribed in a future that was already present; his duplicated language has the strange power of splitting the subject, making it maintain several discourses at once. Language seems to escape the mode of being of discourse and the dynasty of representation. Here, literature is not language approaching itself, but it is rather language getting as far away from itself as possible. It is in this setting, in this outside setting that language unveils its own being. We are sitting on the edge of an abyss that had long been invisible: the being of language only appears for itself with the disappearance of the subject.

How to gain access to this strange relation? Dare we suggest any representation of this subject? Does this tragic hero called Lear reveal what he conceals, or is he only a pure outside, equivalent to a darkness that disperses, like a blown out candle? Is Lear's negligence and lack of discipline a way of manifesting or concealing the law, a way of manifesting the withdrawal with which it conceals itself, and consequently attracting it in a light that hides it? Where then would law power reside, and by what force or prestige would it command respect? Is the presence of law in its concealment? Maybe the law that Lear symbolises is only a shadow, a shadow toward which every gesture necessarily advances; it is itself the shadow of the advancing gesture. There exist good reasons to show that there is a certain absence to be supplemented in the text of the play, and in its textual subject. Lear never dies as an "I" in the first person, but as an eye: his failure is that of perception and vision. Lear regains sight and vision only when the bell of death begins to toll. We witness on this level, the way in which impossibility discourses with possibility, madness with reason, actions with intentions, words with thoughts. The very idea of the first person, with all its claims to agency is undermined. The majesty of the sovereign "I" of King Lear is reduced to a storyteller: it is the raving of the lost self which confesses itself: "Does any here know me? This is not Lear:// Does Lear walk thus? Speak thus? Where are his// eyes?// Who is it that can tell me who I am?" (I, iv, 223 – 227)

There is here a whole terminology related to perception, vision, or optics — as opposed to opinion or sentiment. There is an emphasis on body and image space, and a whole spatial dimension is hence introduced. This image space depicted by Lear can no longer be measured out by contemplation: Lear the subject, has entered into this image space by becoming part of it, literally with his body: "Does Lear walk thus"? Here, Lear himself participates in the scene that he imagines. In this schema, body and language form the opposing cardinal points of a semicircle from which the circles of Lear's existence then variously extend. The distinction between the perceiver and the perceived, the naming and the named, and between man and nature has been eliminated in so far as body space and image space are themselves indistinguishable. We are in front of a body that has lost its distinctive boundaries. What is being addressed is a language of the body in which the forgotten, while visible, is not really decipherable: the body as material and matrix of language of the unconscious. It is in this context that we find an image which reads as the reverse side of the notion of body — an image space, an image in which the coincidence of representation and perception manifests itself in the same material, in the body — but as fear.

This is the law that does not want to change, subsiding into the grave once and for all, and each of its forms is only a metamorphosis of that never ending death. This is the name that is being transformed into something unnameable, an absent absence, the amorphous presence of the void and the mute horror of that presence. This is the image of the human self experiencing the void within itself, incapable of filling the void, asserting itself as pure nothingness; a nothingness stated and restated by a subject that is the agent of its own instability: in Kafkian terms, Lear is "a cage looking for a bird." Shakespearean metamorphoses seem to take place within the mind, even when they are imposed from within. But we usually know that a metamorphosis takes place when identity breaks down; it is the process we see Lear undergoing from Act III, scene iv, onwards. In that sense, Lear begins to lose a sense of his own self, then by the time he exists, the image of metamorphosis is explicit in: "Thou shalt find// That I'll resume the shape which thou dost think// I have cast off for ever" (I, iv, 306–308). This involuntary psychological metamorphosis is accompanied by Edgar's controlled, if forced transformation into Poor Tom through disguise: "I will preserve myself; and am bethought// To take the basest and most poorest shape// That ever penury in contempt of man// Brought near to beast"; (II, iii, 6–9).

We are facing here a very delicate philosophical problem: instability and change. Change itself becomes constancy, and instability a fixed principle. This means that there is an essence in both human and non-human nature, and that there is also an infinite variety of human passions and actions. Freud, as we know, held that there is no "no" in the unconscious and that when a person negates or denies communicating a thought to him, it is a sign that he cannot accept the contents of the thought, or can only admit them into consciousness in the form of a denial. "Does Lear walk thus"? To put such a question is already to answer it. Here, it is the body that is put into question. Is there, or can we imagine that a person is not identical to his body? To say that a person is not identical to his body is to take issue with the materialist possibility that a person is identical to his body. Are we ever called upon in the stream of life to wonder whether someone either is or is not identical to his body? Are we ever called upon to distinguish between the two? Why is Lear so worried about his walking and his gait? Does he live in the body, and consequently sees with the body's imagination things in outline? Does a fully dimensioned seeing take place outside of his body? Is Lear undergoing then a gradual transformation? Does the question "Does Lear walk thus" have an intelligible role to the play?

I submit this could be nothing but a conceptual joke and such a joke can be very instructive. Of course this statement makes clear the King was dead, while leaving open the possibility that he was still alive. This shows also that the crossing out erases nothing, that it is impossible to deny without simultaneously re-inscribing. In a somewhat similar vein, we can imagine that Lear was gazing upon his body prepared for burial. To tell the truth, there is more in that than merely a colourful way of remarking that the old king is dead, for he speaks of all that once was and no longer will be. This person/body distinction is not distinction between life and death, nor anything that is captured in the expression of remembrance and grief and perhaps even of hope. To refer to the body in such a situation means to renounce something, or more precisely to denounce something. But it is the word and not the body that has the attitude here. The body serves only to cover up the real word. It is the masquerade of the language that dissimulates language. Says Deleuze: "Le langage est un œuf en voie de différenciation. Le corps cèle, recèle un langage caché; le langage forme un corps glorieux [...]. L'acte du langage fabrique un corps pour l'esprit, l'acte par lequel le langage ainsi se dépasse en réfléchissant un corps. Transgression du langage par le langage." (Deleuze, *Logique* 325 – 326)

It seems that Shakespeare, through a sort of semanalysis, attempts to bring the speaking body Lear – complete with drives – back into language. This means in a way that the logic of signification is already present in the material body. As a matter of fact, the body is on display from the very beginning of the play, even though it is presented so systematically as an object of spectacular violence and torture: we witness the old king threaten to pluck out his "old fond eyes" (I, iv, 301 – 302), Edmund's self mutilation, Kent's feet twisted painfully into the stocks, Edgar and Lear naked on the heath, Gloucester's eyes put out, and finally the corpse of Cordelia in Lear's arms. This manifestation of the body is not of any interest to us. We are interested in the body not as a thing or a substance, but as a continuous creation, and an energy system, which is never a complete structure, never static, but in perpetual inner self construction and self destruction; the body as an object of knowledge.

Throughout *King Lear*, the body is the site of personal identity, a symbol of social order, an open space where we discover the conditions for understanding and knowing. Throughout the play, the body is being transformed from an object of power to a humble dwelling place of the soul. Seen through Lear, the body becomes a space within and upon which insanity is located. It is disrupted, dislocated in masquerades, disguises, counterfeits and dementia. Subversion is its potential. What Shakespeare does, however, is try to show that the disruption of the body, within both subject and state, leads to madness. Faced with madness, or

madness of discourse, the body is completely stripped of power and effective presence. In tragic or genuine madness, the body is openly displayed but lacks power and effective presence. Devoid of normative meaning, the mad body signifies its emptiness through a semiotics of contradiction and disfigurement. Mad Lear, divested of his clothes and his power, may bellow at the wind but all to no consequence. At the same time, the erasure of power from the body in madness heightens the stark significance of that corporeality since, for a time, the mad body is liberated to display the nakedness, the blank, on which all social meaning depends. (Salkeld 61)

There is no doubt that the play derives a considerable corporeal impact from its many references to the body. It seems that a knowledge of the body provides the groundwork for a knowledge of the mind and its states of health or illness. The states of mind displayed in this play are mere transmutations of the body, or the states of body are symbols of the states of mind. Everything is explained and set forth in physiological terms. Corporeal disruption is voiced; corporeality becomes corpus-orality: the reality of the *corps* is transferred to the orality of the *corps*. The body is an open text where we may read the signs of insanity. In other words, the body constructs and deconstructs itself into writing, or more precisely, dismembers itself into writing. It becomes the site where the marks of madness are written. Madness itself does not really occur within the minds of Lear or Edgar — though one's madness is real and the other's is feigned — but in their discourse and above all on their bodies, and both madnesses are mediated by the same corporeal conditions of representations. The play as a performance becomes increasingly at odds with itself through a misprison of identities, and consequently the social body itself experiences the pain of dislocation. The representation of Lear's inner disorders is entirely built up by a series of wider confusions and infusions rampant throughout the play, and brought up raw at the level of the social body. The central image of the play – as Caroline Spurgeon said a long time ago – is that "of human body in anguished movement, tugged, wrenched, beaten, pierced, stung, scourged, dislocated, flayed, gashed, scalded, tortured, and finally broken on the rack." (Spurgeon 339)

The body is a continual hallucination for Lear: he gives violent voice to anger directed mainly against the female body. When Goneril denies her father his train of "a hundred knights and squires," Lear prays heaven and earth to make her sterile, "a derogate body", and "create her child of spleen that it may live and be a thwart disnatur'd torment to her" (I, iv, 280–283). Lear also threatens Goneril with a revenge from Cordelia: "I have another daughter... when she shall hear this of thee, with her nails she'll flay thy wolfish visage" (I, iv, 305–308). Lear condemns Goneril and speaks of her as a "disease that's in my flesh, which I must needs call mine: Thou art a boil, a plague sore, or embossed carbuncle in my corrupted blood" (II, iv, 221–224). The enemy is acknowledged by Lear as an enemy in the blood, in the body. This is to say that Lear's real preoccupation with images relative to the body is not to be interpreted as a kind of fixation — be it Freudian or Jungian — but is rather a confrontation with all the irreducible substance and "hue of resolution/unresolution" which is subjacent in all that is political, philosophical, and juridical in the old order. If — as

Salkeld maintains — for Descartes the body is mutable and an unreliable source of knowledge, for Shakespeare, it solidifies, on the contrary, into the only sure ground for all knowledge, meaning and subjectivity. (Salkeld 105) When Lear embarks on his "dark purpose," and begins to confront once and for all the uncertainties of his world, he repeatedly finds that the palpable substance of the body is itself the very stuff of subjectivity and sociability: "Nature, being oppress'd, commands the mind to suffer with the body" (II, iv, 105). For Lear there is no division of body and soul because, "When the mind's free// The body's delicate; this tempest in my mind// Doth from my senses take all feeling else// Save what beats there – filial ingratitude!// Is it not as this mouth should tear this hand// For lifting food to't?" (III, iv, 11 – 16)

Lear sees in the "uncover'd body," the naked Edgar, the irreducible truth of all truths, the bare material reality of life: "thou art the thing itself; un-accommodated man is no more but such a poor, bare forked animal as thou art. Off, off, you lendings! Come; unbutton here" (III, iv, 104 – 107). The body is nothing but the place where Lear can observe all the hypocrisy, vice and treachery of this world. He may doubt the loyalty of his daughters, he may not trust the moral stability of his world, but he never seems to doubt the durability and endurance of the body, even in hell: "But I will punish home:// No, I will weep no more. In such a night// To shut me out? Pour on; I will endure" (III, iv, 16 – 18). When all certainties begin to fall apart and the truth is transformed into untruth, the only certainty that Lear finds and believes in is "this basest shape," the body. It is the body which revolts against its own organs: "the mouth that tears the hand for lifting food to't." How could we account for this "mouth tearing up the hand for lifting food to it"?

The first thing that comes up to mind here is that the "hand" is in danger. This means in Heideggerian terms that thought itself is in trouble: to think is a handwork says Heidegger, and he says it without any hesitation. (4) To think is therefore a manual work. This does not mean obviously that we think with our hands as we say in French, that we speak with our hands when we accompany our speech with gestures. Why does Heidegger choose the hand then, as a reference to thinking, while elsewhere, he willingly relates thinking to light or to Lichtung, to the eye, and the hearing of the voice?

Heidegger relates thinking to a situation of the body, the human body and to the human being. This means that thinking is not cerebral. The hand thinks before being thought; it is thought. It sends us back to something particular, to a separate substance. Descartes tells us that the hand (5) is part of the body, but it is endowed with such an independence that we can consider it a separate thing by itself, though the body remains always distinct from the mind, and is always a source of unreliable knowledge: "I thereby concluded that I was a substance, of which the whole essence or nature consists in thinking, and which, in order to exist, needs no place and depends on no material thing; so that this "I", that is to say, the mind, by which I am what I am, is entirely distinct from the body, and even that it is easier to know than the body, and moreover, that even if the body were not, it would not cease to be all that it is." (Descartes 54)

For Heidegger, the being of the hand is not determined by its being a corporeal organ of pre-hension; it is not an organic part of the body intended to take, to catch hold of, to claw; it is rather mainly intended to understand taking, mastering and manipulating, to conceive, to understand. Merleau-Ponty's provocative analysis of "le corps propre" (6) goes a step further, extending to the entire body. Merleau-Ponty sees the body as having a telos towards rationality and explicitness. In his most important work, *Phenomenology of Perception*, he situates consciousness in the body. His notion of "perception" as the situated, embodied, unreflected knowledge of the world rejects splitting the mind off from the body or treating the body mechanistically as a mere object. Consciousness is always incarnate, he argues, or else it would lack a situation through which to engage the world. Merleau-Ponty's awareness of the necessary situatedness of existence makes him emphasise the inescapability of social and political entanglements in the constitution of subjects. In his later writing, Merleau-Ponty's project is to bring out the logic of what he calls "visibility." Visibility according to him, arises out of the conjuncture of the visible and the invisible. Visibility is situated at the horizon of the visible. It is both that which arises out of seeing visible things in the world and the condition of the possibility of such seeing. Visibility both identifies visible things as seen, as visible, and distributes them throughout the field of vision. Accompanying visible things is the invisible vision which sees. For Merleau-Ponty, this visibility is located in and passes through the locus of the body. Visible objects surround us, and even enter into us as embodied seers in the world. One's fleshly situatedness in the world makes one particularly susceptible to the sensuous qualities of the texture of things. We see things, we touch things, we feel things — we thereby incorporate them into our daily existence. Visibility is therefore our incorporation of things and that which renders it possible for us to incorporate things.

But if we assume that Merleau-Ponty is correct, how is it that power and organisational rationality are so infrequently linked in other cultures? If on the other hand power and rationality are not grounded in the body's need to get a maximum grip on the world, what is the relation between the body's capacities and power? An answer of this relationship between the hand and power could be found in the oriental approach to this link hand/power. As a matter of fact, for the Arabs the hand is with the heart and the head an essential pole of the nobility of man. The hand is also a very interesting element of the ensemble of the ancient iconography. It is located at the same level as the eye, and no other body organ can exceed it. The hand is also associated with royal strength, domination and royal power. The Hebrew word "iad" (identical to Arabic) means at the same time hand and power. Therefore Shakespeare's hand sends us back to power, sovereignty and royal strength. So if the hand is in trouble, it is in fact royal authority that is in trouble; it is power disintegrating with the organs of the body.

Michel Foucault is another reinterpreter of the notion of body. For him, we may speak of bodies of knowledge, as bodies of desire, institutional bodies, professional bodies and so on. It is the changing body that produces the modern medical body that houses and defines both sickness and health. In *The Birth of the Clinic*, Foucault sustains that as bodies collide, mingle, and suffer, they create events on their surfaces, events that are without thickness, mixture, or passion. And if for Gilles Deleuze, bodies are external to events, for Foucault, bodies are themselves events, and are made up of the effective forces that constitute their histories: "The body is molded by a great many distinct regimes; it is broken down by the rhythms of work, rest, and holidays; it is poisoned by food or values, through eating habits or moral values; it constructs resistances." (Foucault, *Language* 153)

Under such an outlook, Lear's body appears not only describable but also traceable. To posit the system of reading a text is therefore not only to ask and to show that it can be interpreted freely, but it is mainly, and much more radically, to gain acknowledgement that there is no objective or subjective truth of meaning, but only a ludic truth. We can dislodge those affective powers of discourse, typical of Lear, discourses that rely on a certain dominance of ordered identity for interpreting and judging things and characters around him. Next to his self, Lear discovers the existence of another language that also speaks, and that he is not able to dominate, one that strives, fails and falls silent and that he cannot manipulate. The language that he once spoke and has now separated itself from him is now residing in a space increasingly silent. It is language that is indeed directed at contents that pre-exist it; but in its own being, provided that it holds as close to its being as possible, it only unfolds in the pureness of the wait. Relationship becomes intrusion and collusion, just as coherence or recognition. Contestation becomes the rule; but contestation here is not a principle of negation, it is only an affirmation that affirms nothing: "Who is it that can tell me who I am"? (I, iv, 227).

There looms here the metaphor of seeing and knowing. It is philosophy that is interrogating what is called perceptual faith; and when philosophy interrogates, it neither expects nor receives an answer in the ordinary sense. Maybe it is because the existing world already exists in an interrogative mode. Lear's question about his "I" is to be inscribed in the question of self portraiture, and it also says a great deal about the relationship between eye and mind, and the body as both seeing and seen. It is the self constituting itself as other, modifying in the other way Rimbaud's dictum: the *"je" est un autre*. The plan offered in Lear's question is corporeal. The self is embodied, visible, seen. It is drawn out, or extracted through the body, and King Lear becomes, on this level, an agent and a patient: the portrayer and the portrayed. His self is not represented as a soul but as embodied. All traces are here bodily shapes, expressions, ways of walking, glances. In other words, Lear is lending his body to the world of things in order to transform them, and so he takes the visibility of his body for the visibility of the things he wants to change. This is why Lear never stops talking. Dividing himself and yet also bringing together difference, he is embedded in a difference between the semiotic and the symbolic, or between an indirect language and a pure language. And since knowing is also closely associated with seeing things as they are, the light of knowing and the light of reality are deeply linked, and that linkage is supposed to give us an essential affiliation of the light of knowing/believing and the light of being. Lear's body somehow exceeds his memory and his consciousness, creating a confusion that goes so far as to become a doubt: "Who is it that can tell me who I am"? Reading itself is here the gesture of the body, for of course Lear or anybody else in this situation reads with their body, which by one and the same movement posits and perverts its order: an interior supplement of perversion. Lear is living in a state of atrocious strife, a conflict that is related to the question of the self. All depends on the answer, or more precisely, on whether language gives or withholds the appropriate word. Language in its attentive and forgetful being, with its power to dissimulate and efface every determinate meaning, and even the existence of the speaker in this neutrality that constitutes the essential and fundamental place of all being, is neither truth nor time, neither eternity nor man; it is, instead, the always undone form of the outside. It places the original Lear in contact with death, or rather, brings both Lear and his origin to light in the flash of their infinite and close oscillation, a contact in a boundless space. We are dealing here with the "Who" besieged by the problematic of the trace and of "différance," of affirmation, of the signature, and of the so called proper name, of the subject, object and project. Certainly there is a power in asking questions, and this can be explained as Lear's endeavour to re-inscribe himself in an experience of affirmation, because he feels he is dislocated, lacking in firmness and closure. But the only problem is that his consciousness does not coincide with the self. This does not simply characterise a state, a fact, but it is the unknown and sliding being of an indefinite "Who." It is the subjectivity of the hostage. Seen under another perspective, what Lear raises to this high degree is not his personal self, since he has renounced his personality by making it the object of his thought, and since he has given the place of subject to that unqualifiable "I" which has no name, which is neither more tangible nor less real than the "centre of gravity of a ring." The pure "I" or this supposed source of all presence, is thus reduced to an abstract point, to a pure form, stripped of all thickness, of all depth, without character, without property, without an assignable duration. This source has no proper meaning anymore. Nothing of that which proceeds from it belongs to it. Lear the noun is so universal and so abstract that it stands for no proper name of any person in particular. The function of this source which names itself "I" is indeed within but yet outside of language: a relation of nothing to nothing. Imagine this king attempting by himself to describe himself, to catch himself in the grid of a determining discourse: he almost annihilates himself. In order to affirm himself, this name Lear had to begin by denying an infinite number of elements, an infinite number of times, and by exhausting the objects of his power without exhausting that power — with the result that it differs from nothingness, by the smallest possible margin. The "I" is often described as a glance, or as the site of a glance. The eye becomes simultaneously the division that opens and the substance of the source, the point of departure and the point of arrival. It is mirror and lamp: it discharges its light into the world around it, while in a movement that is not necessarily contradictory, it precipitates this same light into the transparency of its well. The eye at this phase is the figure of being in the act of transgressing its own limit; and consequently it reflects at this level the beginning of the disintegration of language, or more precisely the turning back of language upon itself. It is when language, arriving at its confines, overleaps itself, explodes, challenges itself in tears, speaking of itself in a second language, in which the absence of a sovereign subject outlines its essential emptiness and incessantly fractures the unity of his discourse. In Bataille for example, the eye delineates the zone shared by language and death, the place where language discovers its being in the crossing of its limits. Between what Lear says and what he hears himself say, there is no logical link, no exterior reference. There is nothing more astonishing than this interior speech, which is heard without any noise and is articulated without movement. Everything comes to be explained and thrashed out in this circle, like a snake biting its tail. The existence of the speech from self to self is the sign of a real wound. Lear's mind — shall we say in Woolfian terms —keeps throwing up from its depths, scenes, sayings, memories and ideas like a fountain spurting over that glaring, hideously difficult space. It is a real poetic language both in its roots and in its process of creation; a gigantic machinery which marks the points of indifference between creation and destruction, dawn and death. It also says a great deal about this invisible depth of Shakespeare's language, which communicates vertically with its own sustained destruction. This is the mobilisation of possibility, which realises too late its essential rapport with impossibility; and realises also that its wavering trajectory towards failure and purposelessness is its only authenticity.

Lear's daughters, Goneril and Regan will suddenly represent "l'interdit," the fore bidden, which marks the point where power ceases, as Blanchot would say. Lear bereft of power, is beyond reach, a metaphor of the inaccessible, the *franchissement de l'infranchissable*. The only resort left for Lear is to lose himself in rhetoric, forsaking real understanding: "This is the epitome of Lear's self-delusion, betraying a complete misunderstanding, or more exactly, a vehement refusal to understand, what he is and what he is not. The fragmentary thoughts that break into his self-absorption depict a mind being dragged unwillingly through a world, it is no longer sure of, pushed toward consequences it can foresee but not forestall. His state of mind is characterised by alternation between various different approaches to the situation, the kind of fragmentation which in Shakespeare's world is synonymous with the destruction of the subjective world."(7)

Shakespeare sees Lear in this fragmented universe as the symbol of the destruction of the subjective world. He introduces a faithfully self conscious prose that is radically self aware of its subjectlessness, characterlessness, a voice of the unnameable, reduced to mere words, this dust of words uttered by Lear, with no ground on which to settle, no space in which to disperse; words coming together, moving apart, fleeing one another, merging with one another, yet never meet. They are a voice with no source, a non localised voice; the voice of a ghost that is seeking its place. The upright pronoun "I" does not represent any subject, but the void subject position, thrown in a dizzyingly detached anti-space: "an O without a figure." This "I" calls into mind Woolf's *A Room of One's Own*. Woolf states at the beginning of *Room* that she "will be making use of all the liberties and licences of a novelist in her lectures and that the 'I' is only a convenient term for somebody who has no real being." She notes: "a straight, dark bar, a shadow shaped something like the letter 'I'," which makes it hard "to catch a glimpse of the landscape behind it," and she continues "But [...] the worst of it is that in the shadow of the letter 'I' all is shapeless as mist." (Woolf, *A Room* 6)

In *King Lear* – a play where the dispersal of the self is evident – Shakespeare operates as the ironist of discourse, putting his perpetual motion machine, into action, poised at the threshold of the abyss, forcing us to rely on those substantial and unsubstantial words. In this transgressive fragmentation of language, the door of the real signified can only be opened, transgressed, forced or broken in. Maybe this is the dialectics of limitation and limitedness of the possible and the impossible. It may also be a resistance to the interpretation of Shakespeare's play: that unreadability or supplication and longing for meaning; calculations without ends.

Transgression in *King Lear* is hence that spectacle in which we witness the illegal without committing it. It does not seek to oppose one thing to another; it does not transform the other side of the mirror; it is neither violence – in an already divided world – nor a victory over limits; its role consists in measuring the excessive distance that it opens at the heart of the limit and to trace the line that causes the limit to rise. In writing, that is to say in the play, transgression leads finally to sacrifice, in which death itself is transferred to a figurative other: Cordelia dies before Lear. Once again, we are presented with the real as a withdrawing excess, a radical disjunction, where language breaks down.

PART TWO
THE POETICS OF THE SILENT LANGUAGE
AND WILL POWER

O good old man, how well in thee appears
The constant service of the antique world,
When service sweat for duty, not for meed.
Thou art not for the fashion of these times,
Where none will sweat but for promotion,
And having that, do choke their service up
Even with the having; it is not so with thee.
As You Like It

Those in possession of absolute power can not only prophesy
        and
make their prophecies come true, but they can also lie and
        make their
lies come true.
Eric Hoffer

A cock has great influence on his own dunghill.
Publilius Syrus

Different attitudes towards the problem of language are distinguished in the use of the word play "Nothing" and its relentless repetition throughout *King Lear*. "The quality of nothing," according to Gloucester, "hath not such need to hide itself. Let's see," he commands Edmund, who is displaying his forged letter by concealing it. Gloucester again: "Come, if it be nothing, I shall not need spectacles." (I, ii, 32 – 35)

Examining the letter, Gloucester realises that it is not "Nothing." Paradoxically speaking, to see Shakespeare's "Nothing" we need spectacles. It is the eye that reads and also the ear. In other words, much of the poetry in the play depends on these repetitions. "Nothing" is closely associated with seeing, hence with reading, sight and the loss of it.

Our first reading of this "nothing" is that words are like things, given and received, a somehow reified rhetoric that wins property. Doesn't "nothing" mean in its literal sense that all being is nothing, and presumably a thing can only be worth nothing because and inasmuch as it is already null and nothing in itself? Isn't it true that for us, the word and concept "nothing" usually carries the concomitant tone of a value, namely, of disvalutation? We say "nothing" when some desired, anticipated, sought, demanded, expected thing is not at hand, is not. "Nothing" implies a thing's not being at hand, its not being. So usually, we think of "nothing" only in terms of what is negated. In *King Lear*, "nothing", a word that echoes so sepulchrally throughout the world of this play, does not signify a particular negation, because it can be defined as such and such:

> GLOUCESTER: What paper were you reading?
> EDMOND: Nothing, my Lord.
> GLOUCESTER: No? What need then that terrible dispatch of
>   it
> into your pocket? The quality of nothing hath not
> such need to hide itself. Let's see: come; if it be no-
> thing, I shall not need spectacles. (I, ii, 30–35)

This "Nothing" represents that Edmond has something to hide. It represents fullness rather than emptiness, presence rather than absence:

> FOOL: Then 'tis like the breath of an unfee'd lawyer; you
> gave me nothing for't. Can you make no use of no-
> thing, Nuncle?
> LEAR: Why no, boy; nothing can be made out of nothing. (I,
>   iv, 127–130)

Heidegger seems to admit that "Nothing" has always got something in it, and it is more of a presence than an absence: "Nothingness 'is' for its part not a possible object. To talk about the *nothing* and to pursue it in thought are shown to be projects without object, vacuous word games that furthermore do not seem to notice that they are always flatly contradicting themselves about the nothing they always have to say that the nothing is such and such. Even when we say simply that the nothing 'is' nothing, we are apparently predicating an 'is' of it and making it into being; we attribute what ought to be withheld from it." (1)

We cannot treat therefore the word "Nothing" as the counteressence to "something," especially as far as Cordelia's "Nothing" is concerned. ("Nothing, my lord.") This "Nothing" has a precise meaning. It is rooted in something, not sayable, and contains an "is" within it. Cordelia has a clear, demonstrative and unshakable hold on the truthfulness of her "Nothing." In other words, her "Nothing" has its basic form of judgement and assertion. It sounds like the product of negation, but it is not; it has its logical origin and justification. Apparently it is the "Nothing" of negation, but it is, in fact, a nothing of no-saying. Through it, language becomes what could not be expressed in words. It is not necessarily what is expressed but what is not expressed but held within; a mystery, a marvel or a wonder. It is when there is no way out, no possible solution that the equivocation of words become the possibility of dialogue, understanding and meaning. The movement of words seems to make language.

We see beneath Cordelia's posture the real dwelling place of lack. In Lacanian terms, we would say that there is no woman who is not excluded by the nature of things, which is the nature of words. Isn't Cordelia that stifled voice which represents the simple phonic formation, the one that refuses communication through wordology? Writes Derrida:

C'est dans un langage sans communication, dans un discours monologue, dans la voix absolument basse de la vie solitaire de l'âme qu'il faut traquer la pureté inentamée de l'expression. Par un étrange paradoxe, le vouloir-dire n'isolerait la pureté concentrée de son ex-pressivité qu'au moment où serait suspendu le rapport à un certain dehors [...] Le discours expressif n'a pas besoin, en tant que tel et dans son essence, d'être effectivement proféré dans le monde. Le sens veut signifier, il ne s'exprime que dans un vouloir-dire qui n'est qu'un vouloir-se-dire de la présence du sens [...] L'essence du langage est la conscience volontaire comme vouloir-dire. C'est seulement quand la communication est suspendue que la pure expressivité peut apparaître. (Derrida, *La voix* 22 – 34 – 37)

It seems then that real expressiveness lies in an elsewhere, or more precisely in its suspension; and that the essence of language is related to its outsideness. This space of nothingness can be a positive state that precedes creativity. Though "Nothing" may be connected to sleep or void, and may signal a retreat into oneself, it is linked in Shakespeare to creative power. It is an empty place, but it is a place of potential. "Nothing" is viewed as a presence, a space to be filled. Perhaps the main function of expressiveness and "vouloir-dire" is not to communicate, neither is it to inform or to indicate. Probably Shakespeare thinks that the essence of something is to be found in its non- essence, and that the character of existence may not be interpreted by means of the concept of purpose, the concept of truth. Existence, love, human relationships aim at nothing and achieve nothing; a comprehensive unity in the plurality of occurrences, happenings and events is always lacking. The character of existence is not true, but false. We lack any ground for convincing ourselves that there is a true world. A rebellion against life's fundamental presuppositions: "man would rather will nothing(ness) than not will at all." as Heidegger would say.

An extract to broach the theme of will to power, nihilism, and the "nothing" is well illustrated in Shakespeare's *Troilus and Cressida*:

> ULYSSES: Take but degree away, untune that string,
> And, hark, what discord follows! each thing meets
> In mere oppugnancy: the bounded waters
> Should lift their bosoms higher than the shores,
> And make a sop of all this solid globe:
> Strength should be lord of imbecility,
> And the rude son should strike his father dead:
> Force should be right; or, rather, right and wrong –
> Between whose endless jar justice resides –
> Should lose their names, and so should justice too.
> Then everything includes itself in power,
> Power into will, will into appetite;
> And appetite, an universal wolf,
> So doubly seconded with will and power,

> Must make perforce an universal prey,
> And last eat up himself. (I, iii, 109 – 124)

In Shakespearean tragedy, the market is just such a cycle of consumption and desire, cannibalising a humanity that "must perforce prey on itself,// Like monsters of the deep." (*King Lear*, IV, ii, 49 – 50) What seems worth noticing is that any general explanation of phenomena in terms of will to power is that knowledge is power, or vice versa. Bacon, Nietzsche, and Foucault all after Shakespeare, asserted this, though in different ways. For Nietzsche and Foucault the "is" connecting knowledge and power does not indicate that the relation of knowledge and power is one of predication such that knowledge leads to power. Rather, the relation is such that knowledge is not gained prior to and independently of the use to which it will be put in order to achieve power, — be it over nature or over other people —, but is already a function of human interests and power relations. Nietzsche indicates this stronger claim by identifying the will to knowledge with the will to power, and Foucault accordingly labels what he is studying power/knowledge.

On the other hand, if Marxians think of power negatively — as domination, coercion, manipulation, authority, or, in short, repression — Shakespeare, Nietzsche and Foucault think of power as producing positive as well as negative effects. Power engenders resistance; there is no power without resistance as Foucault says. Power engenders also discipline and control. It calls us for the sacrifice of bodies and to the sacrifice of the subject of knowledge; and from preventing knowledge, power produces it. This suggests certainly that power and knowledge are not to be studied separately. Power, states Foucault, "is always interactional" despite the negative terms traditionally applied to its effects: "it 'excludes,' it 'represses,' it 'censors,' it 'abstracts,' it 'masks,' it 'conceals'." (Foucault, *Discipline* 194) Instead, Foucault asserts, "Power produces; it produces reality; it produces domains of objects and rituals of truth." (Foucault, *Discipline* 194) Thus there are at least two sides to any discourse of power: indeed, there are many discourses of power, not just one.

Power is the most powerful obsession: it was used as the devil's last throw to tempt the "Son of God" himself. The devil took Jesus up to a high mountain and showed him "all kingdoms of the world and all the glory of them." He then said, "All these will I give thee, if thou wilt fall down and worship me." This story, in St Matthew's Gospel, takes us to the root meaning of obsession. Originally, it was a military term. Obsession was the laying siege to a city or fortress. Then, like many military terms, it was taken over by Christianity to describe an aspect of the eternal war between good and evil. In this sense, it was the process by which the devil besieged man's soul and, if he were triumphant, led him to act wrongly. Then, it was left to our more secular age, in which the psychologist has displaced the priest, to give it its present meaning. Now it is not evil spirits but ideas or passions that, like the devil, are seen as taking over man and possessing his mind. But the most tempting offer is power. When offered all the kingdoms of the world, Jesus was able to say, apparently without pause, "Get thee behind me, Satan." Thomas Hobbes, one of the greatest and darkest of philosophers, thought that the appetite of power is fundamental to our humanity. Instrumental power is our capacity to command the powers of others. And the greatest of these collective human powers is the power of the state, in which the power of its myriad diverse members is combined into a single sovereign will. That is why political power is the ruling passion. And that is why, once acquired, so few are willing to give it up. Caesar had the satisfaction of being assassinated in the plenitude of his power, Margaret Thatcher, the Iron Lady, wept when she drafted her resignation speech. Even Napoleon, who was normally as decisive in speech as in writing, became as loquacious and repetitive as an old man when defeat stared him in the face: "From the sublime to the ridiculous there is only one step," he said over and over again. There is, as a matter of fact, a certain power in listening, as well as in speaking. The spaces of silence and talk, listening and speaking subjects, are part of a discourse of power, dependent on one another.

In *King Lear*, Shakespeare has also given us an answer to the question of being, as the being of beings. I personally do not find that his thought thinks being from its truth as the essential occurrence or being itself, in which being is transformed and whereby "it loses its name." Being, so it seems, is determined as value and is consequently explained in terms of beings as a condition posited by the will to power, or will and power, by the being as such. By claiming that "Strength should be lord of imbecility," "power into will and will into power," Shakespeare is admitting that willing is nothing but striving for something, and that power is the exercise of force. Force, which means also power, speaks essentially through the idiom of blood, and a society of blood means the glorification of war, the sovereignty of death and honour of crime. What will to power or will and power means is so clear that one hesitates to furnish a special explanation for this conjunction of the words. Will to power is evidently striving for the possibility to exercise, striving for possession of power. Yet will to power expresses a feeling of deficiency. The will to is not yet power itself, because it still does not explicitly hold power. The strife of Lear's daughters, Regan and Goneril for example, is a proof of this. This has nothing to do with Nietzsche's "Will to power" for it is considered in his philosophy the basic character of life. With Nietzsche, even being a servant is still a form of will to power, and will to power is the overpowering of power. It means in this case value thinking. As for Shakespeare, striving for power just for the sake of power can only lead to rot and death. With power, there is no inherent logic of stability. At the level of practice, there is a directionality produced from petty calculations, clashes of wills, meshing of minor interests. It is not the essence of power that seems to interest Shakespeare, but how power operates, its diagram of mechanism, its political figure, and its polyvalence when it is applied. Power is always sought after; power acquired becomes appetite. Anyone can manipulate power as long as he/she is in the correct position, and anyone could be subject to that manipulation. As in *King Lear*, power locates, excludes, secludes, exiles, separates; it throws brothers against brothers, fathers against sons and sons against fathers; it is an act of massive, binary division between one set of people and another. Power is the fear of the normal transferred to the abnormal. It operates through a reversal of visibility, striving for the greatest visibility, and its main function is to increase control. It is the machine in which everyone is caught: those who exercise the power as well as those who are subjected to it. In this way, power is a kind of discipline; it disciplines those who exercise it, just as those who are submitted to it. It disciplines individuals, operating on their souls, involving thus all those who come in contact with its apparatus. To say that power is a kind of discipline, means that it punishes, or more precisely, it punishes in order to discipline. "Force should be right, or rather right and wrong ... between whose endless jar justice reside": an extremely thorny problem, that of truth and power. Shakespeare does not seek to reduce knowledge to a base in power nor to conceptualise power as a coherent strategy. He attempts to show the specificity and materiality of the interconnections of will, will to power, truth, justice and knowledge.

Through interpretive analytics, Shakespeare has been able to reveal the concrete, material mechanisms which have produced this reality, describing with acute details the transparent masks behind which these mechanisms of power are hidden. "Power into will, will into appetite, an universal wolf," means in plain words that the quality of the will to power is precisely growth, and its achievement is its cancellation. In order to be, will to power must increase with each fulfilment, making this fulfilment only a step to further oneself. The vaster the power gained, the vaster the appetite for more. When you achieve it, there is "Nothing" there. Nietzsche's famous sentence in *Daybreak* comes into mind: "Not necessity, not desire — no, the love of power is the demon of men. Let them have everything — health, food, a place to live, entertainment — they are and remain unhappy and low spirited: for the demon waits and waits and will be satisfied." And also Hamlet's "Madness in great ones must not unwatched go."

Talking about power, truth, will to power, knowledge, appetite, madness, Shakespeare's position is that truth is not external to power. There is no recourse to objectivity, no recourse to pure objectivity. We have only cultural practices, and these practices have made us what we are. Our main job is not to submit truth to the domination of power, but to free truth from power, and to make all this account function differently within a field of different power, a philosophy of un "esprit sérieux." Writes Foucault: "It seems plausible to me to make fictions work within truth, to introduce truth-effects within a fictional discourse, and in some way to make discourse arouse, fabricate something which does not yet exist, thus to 'fiction' something. One 'fictions' history starting from a political reality that renders it true, one 'fictions' a politics that does not yet exist starting from a historical truth." (Foucault, "Interview" 75)

Power, in the way Foucault sees it, closely linked to domination, does not require a clearly demarcated perpetrator, but it does require a victim. It cannot be a victimless crime, so to speak. Perhaps the victims also exercise it, also victimise others. But power needs targets. Something must be being imposed on someone, if there is to be domination. Perhaps the person – Lear for example – is also helping to impose it on himself, but then an element of fraud, illusion, false pretences, must be involved. So in the case of Shakespeare, it is quite clear that power engenders violence, and hence imbecility, or imbecility and hence violence. A relationship of violence forces bends, destroys, and closes the door on all possibilities. In itself, the exercise of power is not violence, but a total structure of actions brought to bear upon possible actions: it incites, it induces, it seduces, it makes easier or more difficult; in the extreme, it constrains or forbids absolutely; a real set of actions upon other actions. In Shakespeare, power exists in its expression, and expression is not only the manifestation of power, but its reality. Power is more than its expression. It possesses potentiality, and it is not only the cause of a particular effect, but the capacity, wherever it is used, to have that effect. So any analysis which uses the notion of power must also leave a place for freedom and truth. This signifies also that power belongs in a semantic field from which truth and freedom cannot be excluded. Because it is linked with the notion of the imposition on our significant desires, purposes, it cannot be separated from the notion of some relative lifting of this restraint, from an unimpeded fulfilment of these desires and purposes. In other words – and *King Lear* shows this very clearly –, power cannot be known or measured in terms of its expressions, but only experienced as an "in-dwelling." Gadamer seems to share the same concept, when he writes that, "The observation of an effect always shows only the cause, and not the power, if the power is an inner surplus over and above the cause of a given fact. This surplus, of which we are aware in the cause, can certainly be understood also in terms of the effect, in the resistance it offers, in that offering resistance is itself an expression of power. But even then it is through an awareness that power is experienced. Interiority is the mode of experiencing power because power, of its nature, is related to itself alone." (Gadamer 205)

Most of our contemporary writers, especially those who haunt us from our daily awakenings until our troubled sleep, those who govern our approaches, even if we most of the time do not fully accept their theses, seem to take it for granted that power, in order to perpetrate and expand, needs infinite resources, and an intelligent fiendish will. I do not think that Shakespeare agrees with this thesis. On the contrary, for him, power, wherever it is, is perpetually threatened, because it is tempted by its own destruction. It is the self-destruction of authority in all its forms, and abdication is its last aspiration.

As for knowledge, or more precisely, self knowledge in Shakespeare, I think it has a great deal to do with acknowledging the depths to which one will sink, the lengths to which one will go, the ways in which one will abase oneself, in order to maintain the illusion of propriety, importance or safety: "On my knees I beg// That you'll vouchsafe me raiment, bed, and food." For many of Shakespeare's heroes, self knowledge is a mortifying business. It brings them most of the time, to the bitter realisation that the self is founded on emotional chaos and, behind that, emotional deprivation.

Language and death direct the play of *King Lear*, where they join one another, in order to show that they separate. Even sleep is seen here as a "kind assassin" that shuts off the brains, and prepares for those "fresh garments:"

> DOCTOR: Madam, sleeps still. (IV, vii, 13)
> DOCTOR: So please your Majesty
> That we may wake the King? he hath slept long. (IV, vii, 17 –
>   18)
> GENTLEMAN: Ay, Madam, in the heaviness of sleep
> We put fresh garments on him. (IV, vii, 21 – 22)

A picture of life that is so dismal and meaningless emerges here that the only possible hope is for death, which is at once a kind release, and a violent consummation of this intense fear. It is almost irresistible to psychoanalyse this situation, inserting it in what Freud called the "death-drive," which is both aggressively self defensive and self annihilating, and which strives for the ultimate repose or security in death or non-existence. It is impossible on the surface to imagine for long the nothingness of sleep, death, or negation without something coming to mind. In the same light, the aspect of life that is repeated in death is death itself. There are scenes in *King Lear* where death is played upon, imitating life, imitating death in a manner as vivid as it was lived in life: "LEAR: Where have I been? Where am I? Fair daylight?// I am mightily abus'd. I should e'en die with pity// To see another thus. I know not what to say.// I will not swear these are my hands: let's see;// I feel this pin prick. Would I were assur'd// Of my condition!" (IV, vii, 52 – 57)

"Where have I been? Where am I?" What is past and also what is to come become present, namely as outside the expanse of unconcealment. In other words, what presents itself as non-present is what is absent: "Would I were assur'd of my condition!" There are these barriers that repeat life in death and in life what was already dead, a passage of life to death: "pour que Lear à la fin se révèle lui-même, il devrait mourir, mais il lui faudrait le faire en vivant, en se regardant cesser d'être." (Borch-Jacobsen 117)

There is no reality that corresponds to signs; no signature that refers to its word. Only Cordelia, in her dialogue with Lear, tried hard to reconcile the word with the fact. There seems to be a conflict between Shakespeare's self doubts and a certain faith in his own artistic achievements: a conflict between mistrust of poetry as a mere world of words, and the vindication of poetry as the only creative mode of language. There is also this equivocal quality in Shakespeare's poetic language, which always appears teasingly inaccessible; it gives as it takes away, folding back on itself the moment one begins to understand, so that an exactly opposite meaning begins to seem plausible. This world of words seemed to Shakespeare tragically incompatible with the world of things. The moments of apparent personal connection between the poet Shakespeare and his reader are immeasurably enriched by the understanding they share that each must finally remain an irresolvable mystery to the other. We enter that ambiguous realm of address where two people have become one, yet remain irremediably distant from one another.

We all know that the first use of language as a social institution is communication. When language does not function as an instrument of communication, its rational ordination leaves it, and the meaning gets lost. If we examine, for example, the dialogue that Lear pre-establishes with his daughters, we suddenly realise that there is no communication code between Lear and his daughters. He is the one who defines a priori his own code. He predefines the meaning of words and the answers he wants to have. Thus, in creating his own linguistic code, Lear is divorced from language, and consequently shows the first symptoms of madness. It is Lear who establishes the necessary contact for communication: "Know that we have divides// in three our kingdom." So all at once, Lear commits himself to this very communication as addresser and therefore, his daughters become mere addressees. From then on, a certain circulation of messages become possible. This circulation of messages should imply – as an undeniable consequence – a perpetual and automatic reversal of the role that every protagonist occupies within the process of communication. This reversal of roles is what we would properly call exchange. But if we consider that every normal communication supposes at least an exchange of information between the interlocutors, it becomes clear that what is established between Lear and his daughters is not communication but a one way communication. Any answer that does not abide by the pre-established code that Lear coined himself, is not received; it is only rejected and flatly denied. This may explain Lear's misunderstanding of Cordelia. There is a feeling, almost kept under lock and key, that even if the despair is total, the control remains. Truth is to be found in limitation, and passion in despair. What Cordelia conveys in her message is the true expression of her inclination towards duty and pondered love; in the meantime Lear has already fixed the answer he wants to receive: "Which of you shall we say doth love us most"?

It is quite clear then that Cordelia's message is not decodable within Lear's register. Cordelia sounds faithful because she values her role (what society expects from her) of addressee. On this level, we must admit that it is Cordelia who represents the silent "I". She is silence in flesh and blood, quietness par excellence; the real aside: "CORDELIA: [Aside.] What shall Cordelia speak? Love, and be// silent." (I, i, 61 – 62); "CORDELIA: [Aside.] Then poor Cordelia!// And yet not so: since I am sure my love's// More ponderous than my tongue." (I, i, 75 – 77)

With an acute and righteous intuition, Cordelia reverses completely the rapport commonly admitted between poverty and wealth, awkwardness and eloquence. Writes Sylvie Germain:

La vocation de Cordélia est d'aimer contre vents et marées, voilà tout... De rien, tout peut advenir. En premier lieu le malheur: la ruine, l'outrage, le banissement et la malédiction paternelle frappent Cordélia comme la foudre. Elle ne cherche pas à se défendre; elle a pris le risque de la plus folle des franchises, elle en assume les désastreuses conséquences. Car, aussi injuste et douloureuse soit la disgrâce intérieure qui anime et soutient Cordélia... De rien vient donc aussi beaucoup à Cordélia: la reconnaissance et le respect des justes. Mais elle n'en tire nulle vanité, elle reçoit le bien comme elle accuse les coups du mal, avec pudeur et dignité. De rien lui viendra également la mort. Mais n'a-t-elle pas par avance consenti à tout, au nom de cette vocation qui est la sienne – aimer absolument? (Germain 79 – 80)

Cordelia's love is without any compromise, without guarantee, reward or award: "CORDELIA: Unhappy that I am, I cannot heave// My heart into my mouth: I love your Majesty// According to my bond; no more nor less." (I, i, 90 – 92)

Her silence is neither resignation nor submission. It is meditation, a way of being and thinking that frees her from the objectivation or the reifying of the world and the self, and it is the result of representational thinking. It is a way in which human beings are involved directly and immediately in being. It is an awareness of the field, an awareness of the horizon rather than of the objects of ordinary understanding. Cordelia's silence is in this way not submissive to authority, but rather outside authority; it is outside the word and outside writing. Her uncanny reply to Lear shows that, by virtue of his paternal and royal authority, Lear, although soliciting his daughters' expression of love, can be symbolically seen as its censor. In saying precisely "Nothing," Cordelia addresses her father with the only authentic love letter:

> CORDELIA: Nothing my lord.
> LEAR: Nothing?
> CORDELIA: Nothing.
> LEAR: Nothing will come of nothing: speak again.
> CORDELIA: Unhappy that I am, I cannot heave
> My heart into my mouth: I love your Majesty
> According to my bond; no more no less. (I, i, 86 – 92)

Here, Lear's insistence upon explicit verbal statement through words alone, confirms for a fact the reductive mode of his world view, a view unable to cope with dimensions of experience, lying beyond the reach of the straightforwardly expressible. In a world of sound and fury, silence, or the use of non verbal or kinesic modes of communication seems merely uncommunicative. Writes Terence Hawkes, about this verbal withdrawal and this drama nothing/ noting:

The body, after all, talks. In fact, it is of the essence of drama itself, as well as of oral communication at large, that we take up the responsibility to 'note' the body's 'kinesic' contribution as an adjunct to and a moderation of whatever words say. This aspect of language had already perhaps received one of its clearest definitions in an earlier play of Shakespeare's whose very title embodies the pun. In *Much Ado About Nothing*, the capacity to 'note' the silent dimensions of communication turns out to be crucial to the story. In fact, the inability of Hero's accusers to 'note' beyond the level of mere words is the basis of the false accusations that lead almost to tragedy. Only the Friar, who has 'noted' her correctly, observing, for instance, the kinesic import of her blushing, can save Hero from disgrace and death. As he says,

> I have only silent been so long,
> And given way unto this course of fortune,
> By noting of the lady. I have mark'd
> A thousand blushing apparitions
> To start into her face, a thousand innocent shames
> In angel whiteness beat away those blushes,
> and in her eye there hath appear'd a fire
> To burn the errors that these princes hold
> Against her maiden truth. (*Much Ado About Nothing*, IV, i, 156–64)
>   (Terence Hawkes, *William Shakespeare* 54)

Cordelia's use of the word "bond" is intended, in the main, to distance her as far as possible from her elder sisters. "According to my bond" – thinks Nicholas Visser – stands for far more than the inflated protestations of Goneril and Regan; it is part of what became, in the commentaries on imagery and themes that dominated Shakespeare studies for so long, the "Great Bonds" of affect, duty and reciprocity that supposedly bind together families, courts and whole societies. These bonds are seen as the central conception of the play. So in speaking of her bond, Cordelia expresses her real feelings in a "most matter-of-fact metaphor" from the world of business and law, as Heilman would say. In a word, the "bond" that Cordelia speaks of is of no economic consequence whatsoever. It is a "bond" and nothing else. "Nothing my lord" means no present; it is not time to say it. Any answer — as Paul Valéry sustains — "qui n'a de sens que dans l'enceinte du langage répond à une question qui n'est que des mots." This is the main reason why Cordelia avoids answering through words, which express only words, but not thoughts. Time as "nothing" can be thought only according to the modes of time, the past and the future. As being and present are synonymous, to say "nothing" and to say time are the same thing; to say "nothing" in this case is to avoid the discursive manifestation of negativity. The now is always the other, and time is not composed of course of nows: the unity and identity of "now" are problematic, because the "now" cannot unite the sense to the presence of the sense. This is why Cordelia does not yield to the "now" or to the immediate answer, knowing that the "now" serves only calculation, and hence, the possibility of co-existence is the space of the impossible co-existence. This is a real break in the movement of meaning that Lear is not expecting, and which becomes counter meaning. Cordelia refuses the words of auction sale ("no more no less"). At this point, Shakespeare turns love into products to enhance appearance. He resorts – as Hawkes maintains – to this quantitative language of accountancy ("no more no less"), maybe to demonstrate through Cordelia's answers how inadequate a measure this is for the intangible character of human affection. In a Platonic spirit, Shakespeare insists upon the deceptiveness of those finites that constitute our material world, so that we delude ourselves if we limit the realm of human attachments to the counting of tangible goods. What is central here is the rejection of quantity, of number, as a measure for an older faith that transcends it: love "is the star to every wandering bark,// Whose worth's unknown although his height be taken" (Sonnet 116). Again in the beginning of Sonnet 87, Shakespeare puns on the word "dear" in which any thought of the "dear" of affection must be subordinated to the "dear" of the merchant:

> Farewell, thou art too dear for my possessing,
> And like enough thou art know'st thy estimate:
> The charter of thy worth gives thee releasing;
> My bonds in thee are all determinate.
> For how do I hold thee but by thy granting,
> And for that riches where is my deserving?
> The cause of this fair gift in me is wanting,
> And so my patent back again is swerving.
> Thyself thou gav'st, thy own worth then not knowing,
> Or me, to whom thou gav'st it, else mistaking;
> So thy great gift, upon misprison growing,
> Comes home again on better judgment making.
> Thus have I had thee as a dream doth flatter:

In sleep a king, but waking no such matter. (Sonnet 87)

Love is generous, while the world's "truth is a niggard" that insists on exact measurement ("Which of you shall we say doth love us most?"). Shakespeare is here forcing the language of the wise world's arithmetic to reveal its inadequacy. It is very clear then that he is against this mercantile mind and language, against these limiting conceptions of a world obsessed by the commercial notion of value and its language. Some critics such as Nicholas Visser, Martin Orkin and many others have argued that among the many things *King Lear* may be said to be about, the issue of land – of its control, its ownership, its forms of inhabitation and settlement, its relations to fundamental human needs, its relation to power, poverty – is central. Difference, as the distinctness among worlds, among verbal properties and proprieties, is the appropriate realm of the property owning.

Shakespeare seems to see no alternative but to retreat to a privatised world of personal love, a private utopia, which could remake for the lover the reality that history had made into public goods. It is under this perspective that we can consider Cordelia's silence as the incarnation of her measured and pondered love. For her, love is first of all a duty, and therefore it is useless to shout out one's duty. Her actions are grounded upon love that springs not from obligation, but from duty, and consequently she wants to express herself, not in words, but in actions. She knows for a fact the difference between loving and saying. Cordelia represents not only the threshold, but she is also the key, the golden ray, the blossoming of truth and dignity, felicity and love. For her, a word is capable of separating itself from the visible form to which it is tied by its signification, in order to settle on another form, designating it with an ambiguity, which is both its resource and limitation. At this point, language indicates the source of an internal movement; its ties to its meaning can undergo a metamorphosis, without its having to change its form, as if it had turned in, on itself, tracing around a fixed point (the meaning of the word), a circle of possibilities which allows for chance, coincidence, effects, and all the rules of the game and gaming. Cordelia is the one capable of turning away words from their original meaning, showing that she can turn them again to take on a new one, placing them on a tropological level, producing a series of tropes (asides, nothings, "no more no less"): "CORDELIA: [Aside.] What shall Cordelia speak? Love, and be// silent." (I, i, 61);"CORDELIA: [Aside.] Then poor Cordelia!// And yet not so; since I am sure my love's// More ponderous than my tongue." (I, i, 75 – 77)

What could be worse than to be left gasping in an alien atmosphere, trying desperately to tear sustenance from a cruelly implacable world? "Nothing"? What will dictate the answer to this question? In what milieu of evidentiality, of certitude, or at least of understanding must it be unfolded? Who could interpret the meaning of "Nothing?" It cannot be Lear, for he does not notice any discrepancy between his expectations and what is really happening. It cannot be Cordelia, for she actively produces many of the significations in just uttering the word "Nothing." It cannot be any of the other characters, because no one is in a position to explain or shed light on this enigmatic position. "Nothing" reads as terror struck. Therefore, it must be the text which interprets and the interpretation which textualises. Here, the text as textuality is both interpreter and interpreted:

> GLOUCESTER: What paper were you reading?
> EDMOND: Nothing, my Lord.
> GLOUCESTER: No? What needed then that terrible dispatch
>   of it
> into your pocket? The quality of nothing hath not
> such need to hide itself. Let's see: come; if it be no-
> thing, I shall not need spectacles. (I, ii, 30 – 35)

Lear is a character who seems to promote a great fear of silence. Cordelia's silence is very frightening for him. This may be because silence seems to lack boundaries, and can make Lear feel that he is not in control of the situation. In his eyes, silence conveys emptiness, so it is hard to accept it as real and full, in an environment that commands him to be satisfied and fulfilled at every moment. Cordelia's silence however, has nothing to do with manipulation. It is a commitment, a responsibility, a duty, and a proof of love towards her father. Her silence has substance; it is the presence of "Something." What Cordelia seeks is to rescue silence from the connotation of submission or resignation. So it is silence as a meditation, as a way of being and thinking, and it is only accomplished by a shrinking in of awareness. Cordelia's hesitation to mean, is a way of meaning, which refuses the commitment to a perspective, which is a prerequisite for meaning. Her use of "nothing" is a way of signifying, which does not signify, and a refusal to signify which signifies: this contradiction is both a testimony of the intractable paradoxes of contingency, and an attempt to transcend them. Says Derrida:

Why can't I avoid speaking, unless it is because a promise has commited me even before I begin the briefest speech... From the moment I open my mouth, I have already promised; or rather, and sooner, the promise has seized the I which promises to speak to the other, to say something, at the extreme limit to affirm or to confirm by speech at least this: that it is necessary to be silent; and to be silent concerning that about which one cannot speak... Even if I decide to be silent, even if I decide to promise nothing, not to commit myself to saying something that would confirm once again the destination of speech, and the destination toward speech, this silence yet remains a modality of speech: a memory of promise and a promise of memory. (Derrida "How to avoid" 14–15)

Silence can thus be understood as a modality of speech, or more precisely, a memory of speech, a promise of memory. Many authors have praised silence. Virginia Woolf, notable among them, confronts and narrates silences between islands of speech, and has been always preoccupied with silence and the barrier between the sayable and the unsayable. Distinctions are made in her novels between what is left unsaid, something one might have felt but does not say; the unspoken, something not yet formulated or expressed in voiced words; and the unsayable, something not sayable based on social taboos, or something about life that is ineffable. This silence, or more precisely, this break between word and world, can be seen as a phase when certain aspects of being, as represented in Shakespeare's writing, can only be revealed through various configurations of silence: the use of a series of nothings, asides, metaphors, or even the rhythms of silence. It invites a whole theory of the reading of silence, not for the sake of theory itself, but as a means of engaging the multiple levels and meanings of silence that one encounters in a Shakespearean play. "Nothing," no method, no experiment is forbidden. But trying to read silence or account for the real meaning of these series of Nothings and asides in *King Lear* leads us to ask an enormous quantity of questions: is silence a sign? Is it a floating signifier? Is it a word? Is it a concern, a theme, a figure? Is it symbol? A discourse or a rhetoric? Is it a strategy, a presence or an absence? Does it represent a physical space in the text or an implicit structure? How do we empirically grasp silence? How could a writer make silence with words, and how does a reader read silence? How should we – to quote Felman – read the unreadable? Shall we – as she suggests – "read on the basis of the unreadable, would be, not what does the unreadable mean, but how does the unreadable mean. Not what is the meaning of the letters, but in what way do the letters escape meaning?" (Felman 187)

Such questions seem to subvert their own terms, and I make no attempt to answer them. What I am after is to discover in *King Lear* the many forms of silence, be they voiced or unvoiced, and to explain this rhetoric of silence, this form of writing that has nothing to do with the alphabet, or any codified language. In this discourse of silence, one is more inclined to "try to determine in the different ways of not saying ... things .... There is not one but many silences, and they are an integral part of the strategies that underlie and permeate discourses." (Foucault, *The Foucault* 931)

My real intention is therefore to provide a certain articulation and interpretation of silence, showing that Shakespeare anticipated many philosophical themes that we find in modern thought. One of them is that silence is a symptom or more precisely a sign by which literature draws attention to itself and "points out its mask" as Genette would say. Silence, as understood in modern thought, may possess the same order as the readable, the same order as words on the page! Silence can be used as a technique to capture being, or as a mask that hides that language of the interior, "whirling about" as George Poulet has shown. What cannot be said is then silenced, though it always remains a modality of speech. To avoid speaking implies that there is a secret that could not be manifested, or an emotion that could not be expressed. Kent of course understood the secret intentions of Cordelia, and the promise that her "Nothing" contains. How could a secret be a secret? What should be done in order that a secret be a secret?

The materiality of language is a field that has its dangers and where language exclusion operates. Unless Cordelia's views are presented in a form acceptable to Lear, they will not be given a proper hearing. Cordelia lacks that ability to raise her unconscious thoughts to the conscious level. It is not that she lacks courage; she only lacks that language which cannot betray her feelings, her speech. There is no suitable code that can formulate Cordelia's opinion and her love for her father. Lear, according to Cordelia should not have to be told in words. That is the point and that is the thing that is very hard for word people to believe; that there are other ways of saying and telling. Love in *King Lear*, appears as the negation of negation and in revealing ironically its differential contradictions, it becomes potentially useful knowledge. This is also a proof that self contradictions in language allow no place to speak of love, or any other value, without engaging in a battle of power. In other words, the language hidden in the revelation only reveals that, beyond it, there is no more language and what speaks quietly within it, is already silence: death is the leveller in this last language which discovers within it only its demise. It is the most efficient means by which joining death is identified with discovery. Cordelia's language is located in what it could be called the tropical space of vocabulary. Her speech has organised a space that is full, plentiful, solid, and massive, where "Nothing" can threaten the words, as long as they remain faithful and obedient to their principle and destination. Cordelia has set up a verbal world, whose elements stand tightly packed together, against the unforeseen. Her language refuses sleep, dreams, double dealing, events in general, and seems to hurl this fundamental challenge against time itself. It is a language located on that silent axis where the possibility of language takes shape. It is this absolute distance of language from itself which makes silence speak. Cordelia shows for a fact that at the moment of speaking, the words are already there, while before speaking, there was "Nothing." The process consists, therefore, of purifying discourse of all that false coincidence of inspiration, of fantasy, of the mouth running on by itself, fooling the other. In this regard, Merleau-Ponty writes:

If we rid our minds of the idea that our language is the translation or cipher of an original text, we shall see that the idea of complete expression is nonsensical, and that all language is indirect or allusive – that is, if you wish, silence. [...] If we want to understand language as an originating operation, we must pretend to have never spoken, submit language to a reduction without which it would once more escape us to what it signifies for us, look at it as deaf people look at those who are speaking, compare the art of language to other arts of expression, and try to see it as one of these mute arts. (Merleau-Ponty, *Signs* 43 – 46)

Shakespearean silence is a sign through which literature shows its mask. Through the word "Nothing," Shakespeare seeks to express silence, its nature, its meanings, and its different uses. It is a refined technique to capture the being through nothingness and thus, point out the mask of language. Silence becomes an interior distance, the verbal as well as the non verbal. Maybe the unsaid, which seems to beyond the reach of language, is precisely what founds language – exactitude of the unsaid rather than expressiveness of the said. Cordelia's language is in this way what we could call "langage parlant", and not "langage parlé." "Langage parlant" means that type of language which makes itself in its practice. It is not bound by the established, sedimented elements of an already-constituted language, in which there is a stock of accepted relations between signs and familiar significations. Cordelia's naming is not bound by laws, conventions and established understanding. It is not limited, circumscribed, or constrained by the paternal law, whose symbol is Lear. Her language cannot consolidate, formulate, formularise, or regulate an established meaning; it cannot confirm the mode of speech, embraced by Regan and Goneril. What speaks in Cordelia's silence is another order of sense and expression. Here, the positing, assertive, formal, or systematic features of language are not determinative anymore. Dr. Johnson – as Bloom reported – could not endure Cordelia's death, and was so shocked by it that he could not read again the last scenes of the play. He thought that there was a terrible desolation in the last scenes of the tragedy of *King Lear*, an effect that surpasses anything else of its kind, in Shakespeare or in any other writer. In fact, when Cordelia dies, Lear can only howl, he cannot speak.

There is a modern preoccupation with inwardness, and the use of silence in the narratives of writers, but the motif of the inadequacy of language is actually an ancient one. Apparently, words are unable to express the experience of reality that resides in what we see and feel, but do not talk about. Most of what it is to be said cannot be expressed through the ordinary alphabet, and language — as Derrida sustains — bears within itself the necessity of its own critique. Writes Patricia Ondek Laurence, about the preoccupation with silence and the unsaid in modern literature:

Henry James is obsessed with 'not telling' in *The Golden Bowl*; Samuel Beckett refuses expression in *Malone Dies*; Gustave Flaubert is absorbed with the incidental leading him to 'say nothing' in *Madame Bovary*; James Joyce invents an artist who vows 'silence, exile and cunning' in *Portrait of the Artist as a Young Man*; Harold Pinter dramatises a complex of conventional silences in *The Homecoming*; and Gertrude Stein explains that 'silence is so windowful' in *What Happened*. Ezra

Pound, T.S.Eliot, and Wallace Stevens also employ indirection and silence, using minimal poetic forms to dramatise the limitations of language and withdrawal from a fragmented culture into an interior world. (2)

To all this, we could simply add that the most renowned authors in literature, from Mallarmé to Joyce to Artaud, have presented the multiplicity in language and self through silence: ruptures, holes, blanks, spaces in the text, and all these "blinds of a prison house language." Beckett is great in his refined drama, when he presents us a character, his "feet trapped in concrete and his mouth gagged," staring at the audience and saying nothing. Rimbaud, Lautréamont and Mallarmé, tried to restore to language a certain fluidity and a provisional character; but Mallarmé made of his words acts of private mystery. Henri Lefebvre finds that silence is at once inside language and on its near and far sides; Ionesco goes so far as to admit that a civilisation of words is a distraught and lost civilisation, a civilisation of gossip:

It is as if, through becoming involved in literature, I had used up all possible symbols without really penetrating their meaning. They no longer have any vital significance for me. Words have killed images or are concealing them. A civilisation of words is a civilisation distraught. Words create confusion. Words are not the word (les mots ne sont pas la parole)... The fact is that words say nothing, if I may put it that way... There are no words for the deepest experience. The more I try to explain myself, the less I understand myself. Of course, not everything is unsayable in words, only the living truth. (3)

Certainly we live inside the snares of discourse, and the trappings of speech, but we must not assume that a verbal matrix is the only one in which the articulations and conduct of the mind are conceivable. There are actions of the spirit rooted in silence. Contemplation, concentration, thinking – these are all acts that leave language behind them. In other words, the ineffable lies beyond the frontiers of the word and the spoken. The walls of understanding should break the walls of syntax, in order to reach the purity of the unspoken word. There is here no primacy of the word, no spoken and communicative discourse. Cordelia's reality is in this way a reality which begins outside verbal language. Words imply and engender responsible apprehension of the truth, and we are aware that language is not necessarily a road that demonstrate truth, but is only a gallery of mirrors. There is no link, no verifiable relation between the word and the fact, the word and the thing. What we call fact may be what the Arabs very often call "hijab," a veil spun by language to shroud the mind from reality. Maybe language can only deal with a very restricted segment of reality; the rest – and it is the largest part – is silence. What is usually seen can at any rate be transposed into words, but what is felt more often occurs at some level anterior to language or outside it.

Shakespeare's language, though it seems to control the experienced life, recedes from the communicative grasp of the word. This means, in plain words, that the language has a life of its own, in a sense that goes beyond metaphor, and not necessarily inside language. It is very striking in this regard that in our modern era itself, so much is beyond words. Human talk may have struck dyspeptic Nathaniel Hawthorne like "the croak and crack of fowls," but the rise of language, written and spoken, is all but universally rated as one of the glories of the species. What is surprising is that in the common give and take of daily living, people still rely so little upon the verbal language that distinguishes them from the beasts. In fact, homo sapiens, as a communicator, does not seem to have come all that far from the time when grunts and gesticulations were the main ways of getting messages across. Both individuals and groups still send vital messages by gestures, by pantomime, by dramatics – by a dizzy diversity of what scholars call nonverbal communication. The reality is easy to overlook in an epoch – ours of course, and not Shakespeare's – that is bloated with pride in its dazzling technical marvels of communication. Yet, in spite of human garrulousness, perhaps as little as twenty per cent of the communication among people is verbal, according to experts; most, by far, even when talk is going on, consists of nonverbal signals. "Language," said Samuel Johnson, "is the dress of thought." But all over the world people act as though language were a mere costume — and usually a disguise. Everybody tends to mimic that anonymous signaler cited in proverbs: "He winketh with his eyes, he speaketh with his feet, he teacheth with his fingers." The question that imposes itself is: why has language, given its unique power to convey thought or feeling or almost anything else in the human realm, fallen so short as a practical social tool for man?

The confusion of relationships between the characters in *King Lear* is a way of figuring the world, with its own peculiar combinations of organisation and mutability, pattern and openness to variation. These disorders in

Shakespeare's text seem to get at the bottom of meaning, only to show, that fluidity is not an essence, of only one fundamental, invariable kind, and that no particular mode of incoherence can claim authenticity, just because it is not a restrictive order. As a language, Cordelia's discourse makes particular claims, which contest the rights of other discourses: "CORDELIA: Why have my sisters husbands, if they say// They love you all? Happily, when I shall wed,// That lord whose hand must take my plight shall carry// Half my love with him, half my care and duty:// Sure I shall never marry like my sisters,// To love my father all." (I, i, 98 – 103)

Regan and Goneril in this way are true representatives of the bad side of language. They represent this unbearable evidence that cannot master language. Their language is arranged in a circle within itself, hiding what it has to show, flowing at a dizzying speed toward an invisible void, where things are beyond reach, and where it disappears in its mad pursuit of them. It measures, in a keen way, the infinite distance between the eye and what is seen, or maybe between the I and the scene! This language reflects the poorly placed, the imperceptible, the most secret thoughts, the burden of the irregular, and the inability to rejoin even those things that are the most evident. It can be read as a treatise on love and above all, as a treatise on the marvellous torsions of language: "GONERIL: Sir, I love you more than word can wield the matter;// Dearer than eye-sight, space and liberty;// Beyond what can be valued rich or rare;// No less than life, with grace, health, beauty, honour;// As much as child e'er lov'd, or father found;// A love that makes breath poor and speech unable; Beyond all manner of so much I love// you." (I, i, 54 – 60)

What does this oath mean? To say the least, its issue is already violated by the same words it contains; words similar to waves in a sea shell. Goneril's message is void reverberating void; it is only a sound full of fury and hypocrisy, signifying nothing. There is nothing of a metaphor in it. Love is here measured in terms situated out of space and time; it is dearer than sight and liberty. But this is only a masquerade, a disguise, a linguistic dissimulation. For Goneril and Regan, the insolvency of words are fewer in number than the things they designate, and due to this principle of economy, they must tackle on meaning. This is the reason why their speeches do not belong to either space or time. They are meant to disorient Lear, and make him believe in what they say. The subjectivity at work here is a subjectivity which politicises the limits of representation; a subjectivity without being. If language were as rich as existence, it would be the useless and mute duplicate of things; it would not exist. Yet, without names to identify them, things would remain in darkness. This illuminating flaw of language was experienced by Shakespeare as an anguish, as an obsession. In any case, there remains this bare linguistic fact: language speaks only from something essential that is lacking. From this lack is experienced the play of *King Lear*, in the fact that the same word can designate two different things, and the same sentence repeated can have another meaning. From this follows the proliferating emptiness of language, its capacity to say things, all things, to lead them to their luminous being, to place in the sun their mute truth and to unmask them. From that also follows its power to create by simple repetition things never said, nor heard, nor seen. There is the misery and the celebration of the singular, and the anguish before too many and too few signs. All of Shakespeare's work is brought back to this unity of an anguish before language, an anxiety about the nature of language. Things are perceived because things are lacking; the light of their being is the fiery crater where language breaks down. Things, words, vision and death make a unique form, the very same one that we are. Shakespeare appears as the inventor of a language which only speaks about itself, a language absolutely simple in its duplicated being, a language about language, a *métatexte*, enclosing its own sun in its sovereign and central flaw. The anguish of the signified is what has made Shakespeare's suffering the solitary discovery of what is closest to us in our language. It makes his illness our problem. It enables us to speak of him in the context of his own language. This world of absolute language is in a certain way profoundly silent. The impression given is that everything has been said, but in the depth of this language, something remains silent. The yearnings of the heart are presented like mute signs on a backdrop of night. Maybe a lesson can be formulated, which is essential to understand so many openings and closings in the play, so many broken discourses, right up to the issue of speech and silence. There are sometimes rich opportunities for remaining silent, "de se taire parfois est riche l'occasion," as the French proverb goes. Cordelia understood that. How could Cordelia speak to the figure (Lear) that signifies the suppression of what she has to say? This is one of the most pertinent and crucial questions underlying the whole play.

And it is out of this double bind that the play is both recounted and written. Therefore, whatsoever the situation be, any message addressed to Lear can convey only nothingness. Any message is not only erased, effaced, but destroyed in advance. This means that language can never be disposed of absolutely: it plays with the subject that speaks, and with his repetitions and divisions. The meaning is therefore immobilised beneath the endless waves of language. Lear's sentences no longer refer to things themselves, but to their reproduction. Hence, language becomes a thin blade that slits the identity of things, showing them as hopelessly double and self divided, even as they are repeated up to the movement when words return to their identity, with a regal indifference to everything that differs. What makes Shakespeare great is his great understanding of and ability to express the daily human spirit. The abyss between words and meaning is without any doubt a great burden to us all, and Shakespeare expressed it in all his work. This was a by product of his main topic, which was the human condition.

The characters of the tragedy of Cordelia and Lear are all marked with the same sign; each is prey to the same imagination which carries earth and heaven on its head. All the play is woven out of their words, mysterious mirrors of some magic dreams and miraculous events, all evolving around something called power. This rupture, or fissure through which is inserted the repetition of words, is an aspect of language itself, the stigma of power it exerts on objects, and by which it wounds them. The play itself is given to us divided and wounded before its beginning: "LEAR: Give me the map there. Know that we have divided// In three our kingdom."(I, i, 36–37)

This is what Lear has decided: to divide the kingdom, and cut it into three pieces. The meaning of division itself divides. It can be seen as necessity or inevitability; it can be fate in its painful aspects. This division can be what exposes to dissociation, and at the same time it can also be a line of strategy, a profound movement of keeping. From the moment one divides oneself, one always should keep something in reserve; one does not expose oneself all at once to the threat. This differentiation could be a protection, a strategy of living. From this point of view, division is an exposure to suffering, but it is also a measure taken to save and to keep a kind of reserve or holding back. The kingdom becomes a property that Lear cannot re-appropriate. This property signs him without belonging to him. It only appears to the other and it never comes back to him except in flashes of madness, and brings together life and death, hence bringing Lear together dead and alive at the same time. This is unavoidable. But what we could say – though it may seem paradoxical – is that there is apparently no moment in which a decision can be called presently and fully just: either it has not yet been made according to a rule, and nothing allows us to call it just; or it has already followed a rule — whether received, confirmed, conserved, or reinvented — which in its turn is not absolutely guaranteed by anything. Moreover, if it were guaranteed, the decision would be reduced to calculation ("Which of you shall we say doth love us most"?) and we would not call it just. That is why once a decision is made, the undecidable remains caught, lodged, at least as a ghost, but an essential ghost, in every decision, in every event of decision. In other terms, the undecidable is not merely the oscillation between two significations or two contradictory and very determinate rules, each equally imperative; on the contrary, the undecidable is the experience of that which – though heterogeneous, foreign to the order of the calculable and the rule – is still obliged to give itself up to the impossible decision, while taking account of the law and rules. A decision that did not go through the ordeal of the undecidable would not be a free decision; it would only be the programmable application or unfolding of a calculable process. It might be legal; it would not be just. This is what happened in *King Lear*. Lear gave up his power, but he still wanted to exert his power as if nothing had happened. This phantomatology, or ghostliness, deconstructs from within any assurance of presence, any certitude that would insure the justice of a decision. Who can assure us that Lear has made a final decision when dividing the kingdom? That he has not, instead, and through a detour, followed a certain calculation, a cause, a rule, without even thinking for good to stop ruling? We should not forget that Lear represents a position, and position calls for self-conserving repetition, in the sense that conservation in its turn refounds, so that it can conserve what it claims to find. Maybe it is in this differential contamination (give up the kingdom and at the same time keep it), that we should understand Lear's decision. The whole axiomatic of responsibility, conscience, intention and intentionality that govern Lear's discourse is weak, delicate and crude. We can even recognise, in this discourse, Lear's madness about a desire for justice. This is one of the main reasons that the moment of decision is always a moment of urgency and precipitation, acting in the right of non knowledge and non rule. Says Derrida:

It is from the moment one surrenders to the necessity of divisibility and the undecidable that the question of decision can be posed; and the question of knowing what deciding, affirming — which is to say, also deciding — mean. A decision that would be taken otherwise than on the border of this undecidable would not be a decision. Thus the great decisions that must be taken and must be affirmed are taken and affirmed in this relation to the undecidable itself; at the very moment in which they are no longer possible, they become possible. These are the only decisions possible: impossible ones. Think here of Kierkegaard. The only decision possible is the impossible decision. It is when it is not possible to know what must be done, when knowledge is not and cannot be determining that a decision is possible as such. Otherwise the decision is an application: one knows what has to be done, it's clear. (Derrida, "Dialanguages" 147–148)

It follows that to remain undecided means to turn oneself over to the decision of the other. Indecision is, in fact, being unable to decide as a free subject, a free consciousness, and thus to be paralysed. Otherness here is Lear's daughters. But the most decided is the will not to give up one or the other, either fidelity or a certain infidelity, either a certain responsibility or a certain carefreeness. This is what really happened in *King Lear*. Pure and simple fidelity (Cordelia) is death, and so is infidelity (Regan and Goneril). Who has been running the kingdom after Lear's abdication? Nobody. Here, the idea of the self is nothing but a form of inscription in a dynamic language game, which can only come to rest through the failure to think or the agreement to stop thinking. And so, even in the scenes where dialogue seems to take place, Lear does not dialogue properly; most of the time he monologues. Others have never represented for him a source of information. He takes himself for the unique informant, with no need to be informed. But around him, others communicate, plot and conspire. Lear's communication becomes a series of "quid pro quoes", and his words mere monologues. And in the shifting words that contaminate words, Lear tries to grasp the fleeting but inevitable truth about what has happened. From so many things, without any social standing, from so many fantastic records, he slowly accumulates his own identity, through re-memorising what he has done, and what has been done to him: LEAR: Do you but mark how this becomes the house:// 'Dear daughter, I confess that I am old;// Age is unnecessary: on my knees I beg// That you'll vouchsafe me raiment, bed, and food'." (II, iv, 150 – 153); LEAR: [Rising.] Never, Regan.// She hath abated me of half my train;// Look'd black upon me; struck me with her tongue,// Most serpent-like, upon the very heart. (II, iv, 156 – 158)

Regan, asserts Lear, "hath looked black upon me; struck me with her tongue, most serpent-like." The grammar, spelling and structure of this affirmation instantly transports us back to the time when such an affirmation was made. Language works here like a medium conjuring the dead to new life. The past is not only the entrancing and different past, but has become through this alchemy, or materiality of language, also the present. Lear resorts here to memory, or remembrance. Memory is the mental process by which past events, emotions and sensations are logged and recalled. But what is most important is that memory is also the most essential tool that human beings have for carving a meaningful shape out of the rambling, inconsequential happenings of a lifetime. The urge that dominates Lear's exclamation here is this stubborn attempt to negotiate the number of his train, or shall we say, some coherent pathway from past to present to future in order to live in a certain relative harmony. Lear's version of truth is in this way veering too widely from his daughters' accepted mark, and this is why he is labelled old, mad, bad and dangerous. Conversation between the old king and his daughters become like those nightmarish fairground rides that whirl us round and round on the same axis. Lear, wounded, offers not just a moving account of an illness, but a delicate, sensitive consideration of the relationship between memory and identity. Who are we if we can no longer remember anything about ourselves? Who are any of us without history, kinship, and kingship? *King Lear* explores the links that bind a father, a king to his daughters, as well as the gulfs of experience and expectation that divide them. It is in this way that *King Lear* could be read as a series of vanishing memories, realising almost too late that identity is rooted in rootlessness, founded on the immigrant's profound ambivalence towards the past, towards memory itself. It is the rapid sweep toward the past, the arch of memory, going as far back as necessary to return to a complete clear and dark present. We are repeatedly taken back to the starting point which is now fully fledged: "the dark purpose." Lear introduces a visionary dream-like mode of discourse, which constantly moves towards hyperbole or overstatement. Hyperbole distorts the truth by saying too much;

but still, it is not like telling lies, and there is no intent to deceive listeners. Through hyperbole, Lear juggles with the facts and the apparent meanings. This internal division of Lear takes concrete form in the hallucination of the double. The double, as Freud states, is a substitute that had ceased to reassure: derived from the mirror image, the double was originally a means of defence, a protection against fragmentation, a conjuring of death. Within this kind of discourse, the "I" is dispossessed by the so called Other. Lear's language is confused, and it evidences itself in a language confused in both subject-matter and formulation. He has this tendency to class objects not by common similarity, but instead by preference. Writes Mikkel Borch-Jacobsen: "Le moi s'y voit lui-même hors de lui-même, dans une image d'autant plus extranéisante qu'elle est narcissique, d'autant plus aliénante qu'elle est parfaitement ressemblante. Ce qui était propre et vivante identité (ou identification) devient, une fois représenté, ressemblance dépropriante-miroir glaçant, statue figée." (Borch-Jacobsen 63)

This communicative impasse can actually be described as a fundamental disparity between the manner in which Lear interprets (perceives) contexts, and the way in which others of the same culture do. His communication is the result of differential perceptions pressed into different conceptions of language. Lear's past is not what is past; it is something that never stops coming to pass, and to pass by. It is what never ceases to be repeated, as a vanished present. Time lost is time endlessly recaptured as lost, found in the image of loss: "LEAR: Does any here know me? This is not Lear:// Does Lear walk thus? speak thus? Where are his// eyes?// Either his notion weakens, his discernings// Are lethargied – Ha! walking? 'tis not so.// Who is it that can tell me who I am?" (I, iv, 224 – 228); "LEAR: Thou shalt find// That I'll resume the shape which thou dost think// I have cast off for ever. (I, iv, 306 – 307)

Repeated frustration becomes this dazzling contemplation of a slow death, a sickness unto death. Loss becomes here a doorway, opening onto the invisible visible world. And in the hollow of the real, grows a compensatory delirium, born of loss and separation. Hallucination endlessly strives to meet with Cordelia, to recapture the lost object, to re-establish a cosmic harmony. The entire world becomes a symbolic discourse, that Lear interprets according to his desires and fears: "LEAR: Upon such sacrifices, my Cordelia,// The Gods themselves throw incence. Have I caught// thee?// He that parts us shall bring a brand from heaven,// And fire us hence like foxes. Wipe thine eyes;// The good years shall devour them, flesh and fell,// Ere they shall make us weep: we'll see'em starv'd// first." (V, iii, 20 – 25)

We must note here this discrepancy between the image and the world, between seeing and saying, perception and verbalisation, the level of visibility and the function of the name. There is also a discrepancy between seeing and knowing. Seeing is nothing but the order of the signifier (that which is perceived as a conveyer of the signification in the very process of signifying), while Knowing is the order of the signified (that which has been meant; the accomplished meaning that, as such, is mastered, known, possessed). We are also tempted at this point to think that Shakespeare has introduced in the sphere of cognition, a certain distinction between knowing how and knowing that. As a matter of fact, the word know does not necessarily refer to a cognitive process; rather it is a way of making certain claims in certain contexts. Nothing exists which is not visible, and which does not owe its existence to the fact of being seen. What is seen overlaps both the past and the future, creating a temporal vibration, which does not negate, but rather increases their hieratism. A visibility separate from being seen. No interception between the eye and what it sees: the eye is not situated on the same plane as things seen; it cannot impose on them its point of view (sight), nor its habit, nor its limits. It must without any intervention, let them be seen, by virtue of their being; there is invisibility only within its own space. There is a fundamental lack of proportion. The space registered by looking at the real is shadowy, hazy in layers, deep and circled by darkness in the distance. Lear's concentration on the eye, and his various references to it, is very revealing. With Lear, the eye sees only what is not present and it ceases to be a sifter. Writes Derrida:

L'âme, qui exerce sa puissance dans l'œil, permet de voir ce qui n'est pas, ce qui n'est pas présent, elle "opère dans le non-être et suit Dieu qui opère dans le non-être". Guidé par cette psyché, l'œil traverse ainsi le seuil de l'être vers le non-être pour voir ce qui ne se présente pas. Eckart le compare à un crible. Les choses doivent être passées au crible. Ce n'est pas une figure parmi d'autres, elle dit la différence entre l'être et le non-être, elle la discerne, elle la donne à voir, mais comme l'œil même. Il n' y a pas de texte, surtout pas de sermon, pas de prédication possible, dans l'invention d'un tel filtre. (Derrida, "Comment" 584)

To see and consequently to read, is paradoxically not only to perceive, but also not to perceive; it is to determine an area as invisible, as excluded from perception; an area external to visibility. To see is to draw a limit beyond which vision becomes barred. And indeed and throughout the play, Lear's act of reading consists in his imposing meaning or sense both as directive and as direction upon the others. On this level, even the real is certainly distinct from time, but it is also essentially identical with it. What is real is limited, and the Other to this negation is outside it. Therefore, the determinateness in it is self external, and is consequently the contradiction of its being; the abstraction of this externality and unrest of its contradiction is time itself. Time becomes the nothingness or the accident foreign to essence or truth; the discursive manifestation of negativity. We could probably say that time is already suppressed at the moment one asks the question of meaning, when one relates it to appearing, truth, presence, or essence in general. This is why it seems that there is no other possible answer to the question of the meaning of love made by Lear. Love is that which erases love, and this very erasure is a kind of writing which gives time to be read, and maintains it while suppressing it.

Cordelia's answer to love is "Nothing". But it is this "nothing" that gives value to the concept of love. The valuation of the notion of love is in its erasure and effacement. This is evident proof which shows that writing obscures thought; it is not a guise for language but a disguise, though Shakespeare's purpose is above all to entertain. Writing is therefore a trap, and its actions are vicious and tyrannical, despotic, as we would say today. This demonstrates also that the discursive is related to the non discursive, and that non expressed thoughts are not without signification. So in restricting our glance exclusively to the meaning content and the act of meaning, we confine ourselves only to that sphere of speech, whereas we are supposed to extend the meaning of the words, and modify them suitably, so that they may be applied in a certain way to the whole noetico-noematic sphere, to all acts, therefore, whether these are interwoven with expressive acts or not.

Shakespeare himself alludes frequently that words are more like persons than they are like things. In other terms, the concept of truth as the revealing of what is concealed, means, in a way, that the nature of reality and the nature of man are both hidden and revealed; they both appear and withdraw from view, not in turn but concomitantly. Perhaps the text is al-ways off centre, located where the intratextual meets the extratextual and dedefines its borders. Derrida would say in this regard, that context can be heard as *qu'on texte*: that which is rendered text; it is the making part of the text that which is not part of the text and that which remains other than the text. Words are not always related by falling under a definition; rather they form a family united by a complicated set of similarities, overlappings and crisscrossings; sometimes overall similarities, sometimes similarities of detail. Not only do words have meaning in a context, but they acquire it especially in a *qu'on texte*. One sided diet is one of the main diseases of comprehension.

The eye (the view, the "vue", the sight) or more particularly, this leered and squinted vision of Lear opens up a universe without any exit. It com-bines a vertical point of view – which allows everything to be embraced as if within a circle – and a horizontal point of view — which places the eye at ground level, where it can only see what is in the foreground – to such an extent, that everything is seen in perspective, but each thing, however, is seen frontally. By meaning – and this is the most paradoxical thing – every-one is fooled, and remains caught in the wheel of interpretation. Not only the elimination of uncertainty and doubt, but also the acquisition of cer-tainty and clarity about the meaning of what has appeared ambiguous and obscure, is time and again formulated in *King Lear* as an epistemological assertion, a cognitive achievement, a claim to knowledge. Language itself is obscured by this alien image of Lear the cross eyed. Shakespeare's language seems to show here that the visible and the not visible repeat each other in-finitely, and this duplication gives language its significance. It is language itself that widens this gap between what Lear sees and what Lear wishes to see. As a consequence, we can see that the whole tragedy of *King Lear* is organised around a double mystery, the mystery of reading: the spoken reading (Lear does not read well oral texts), and the written reading (Lear is not able to read or decipher written texts, messages or letters). Reading, in this way, establishes its relation not only to language, but also to power; it consists not only of a search for meaning but also of a struggle to con-trol it. Meaning itself thus unavoidably becomes the outcome of an act of violence. This boils down to the fact that reading in itself is an exercise of violence, but not really an act of violence or force. We recognise meaning in a violence that is not an accident arriving from outside law. That which threatens law already belongs to it, to the right to law, to the origin of law. This is what we would properly call the disease of language, that transposition of what was first a simple fact of language into such a dramatic action. Those mysteries of construction in the language of Shakespeare are like those Chinese puzzles, and our impression is that Shakespeare used them to speed up the disintegration of language, in a way comparable to that in which Mallarmé used blanks. Here, it is no longer the imaginary world that we are facing, but the real one, and it is exploding around us like fireworks: "LEAR: No rescue? What! a prisoner? I am even// The natural fool of Fortune. Use me well;// You shall have ransom. Let me have surgeons;// I am cut to th'brains." (IV, vi, 188 – 191)

With Shakespeare, we are stirred by a language that seems on the point of revealing its secrets. The hollowness that opens within a word would not simply be a property of verbal sign, but a more basic ambiguity, perhaps even more dangerous: it would show that a word, like a gaudy cardboard mask, hides what it duplicates, and is separated from it by the slightest layer of darkness. There is this inner awareness, that by reading the words, we are exposed to the unalloyed danger of reading words, which are both different and the same. Each word is at the same time energised and drained, filled and emptied, by the possibility of there being yet another meaning. This infinitesimal but immense distance between statements will give rise to the most familiar themes: torture by language, and redemption by that same language, and the sovereignty of words, whose enigma conjures up scenes like: "LEAR: No seconds? all myself?// Why this would make a man a man of salt,// To use his eyes for garden water-pots,// Ay, and laying autumn's dust. I will die bravely,// Like a smug bridegroom. What! I will be jovial://
Come, come; I am a king, masters, know you that?" (IV, vi, 192 – 197)

Where to locate Lear? Lear is to be located in that neutral space within language, where the hollowness of the word is shown as an insidious void, arid, and a trap: "KENT: See better, Lear; and let me remain// The true blank of thine eyes." (I, i, 158 – 159)

Lear feels that there is beyond the quasi liberties of expression, an absolute emptiness of being, that he must surround, dominate, and overwhelm with pure invention. He does not really want to duplicate the reality of another world, but he wants to discover an unexpected space, and to cover it with things never said before. Under such a perspective, we can even represent another point of view, through another reading: not much rhetorical effort is required to argue that the question of Lear is the question of the subject, the self, the identity. In this sense, the point is very determined. At the same time, this point is so undetermined, so anonymous, so unnameable, that it lends itself to sacrificial substitution: does Lear have to abdicate the throne, in order to know either himself or his true self? Does he have to be the equivalent of his daughters? Does he have to be exchangeable for another, and is he worth another? Does love have to be at the same time calculable and replaceable, determined and undetermined? Is indivisibility indispensable to the maintenance of power and kingship?

Lear cannot be responsible without experiencing contradictions, and contradictory duties. He is not, by any means, confronting a problem, free of contradiction, or indecisiveness. Lear, this sealed mark of division, the dislocated, and dissociated subject, tries to hold together things that do not easily hold together. He represents the proper name, which cannot be reappropriated. He represents the uniqueness of the event that cannot gather itself into itself. Uniqueness does not mean of course an identity with oneself; it is another experience of the name. Lear, giving up his kingdom, and at the same time longing for its whole possession, does nothing but sign the experience of the impossible, of the double bind, that makes an original signature of every ruin. At that point, Lear will have perhaps lost his name forever, his power and unity, and thus, will become a stranger to himself. This is because there is in Lear's language a serious and dark problem of translation, between what can be envisaged for the word, and the usage itself, the reserves of the word. All his sentences are disarranged, decomposed, and undone. He even returns to his sentences, but only to erase them, and not to clarify them. His discourse is a discourse that cannot make up for the incapacity of words, and which remains unequal to thought.

Why does Lear always need somebody to remind him of his name, his titles? Why does he want to listen to his name echoed, reverberated? Is it a desire for nakedness, a desire for this naked name? Maybe it is because the name has to be forged, coined and invented for the self, and especially for others, in order to be re-spectered into the structure of language, and hence, gain its space! Survival of the name! For responsibility to be responsible, one has to try to go beyond the limit, beyond the borderline. Lear in this case needs to be reminded of his name, because his name as a signature is already dead. Here, signature is the written part of language: instead of thinking that he is living at the end of writing, Lear seems to be satisfied with living in the extension, the overwhelming extension of writing, as a figure, or more precisely as an "O without a figure," a phantom, a shadow; and as everybody knows, nobody can jump over his own shadow. Of this person, or of this shadow, what is the measure of the other? Of this visage or of its reflection, which one judges the other? If the shadow remains a shadow, if the reflection is only a reflection, what is the degree of reality that we can grant to the visible? The projection of a shadow or of an image leads us to think of the visible as the place where things divide, separate, unfold, multiply according to the surfaces that reflect them, without breaking the visual continuity. Lear is caught in this closed system, confined and cloistered, unable to loosen his chains. He represents this idea of madness, which at first sight, does not teach us anything about God's power, the idea of power, and of course logos. Lear is, as a matter of fact, shut off, isolated, enclosed by his own power. The letters that make up his name, L.E.A.R., do not really form either a preposition or a proposition in themselves. There is enough in them to engender almost all the hidden meanings contained in the name Lear. In this proper name, a certain urge induces us to think that Lear should be taught to hear with his eyes. This urge is contained in the extracted word EAR, which sends us back immediately to hearing, and which becomes more urgent in the order of Kent to Lear: "See better, Lear."

There is certainly, in this word play, a very clear circular complicity, or an exchange, between the metaphor of the eye (seeing) and that of the ear (hearing). What is at issue is the ear, that distinct organ that approximates and articulates. In order that what Lear decries be heard and understood, he must be subjected and constrained to the law of what Nietzsche calls the "inner hammer." Remember Zarathustra, who was asking himself if he would have to puncture them and batter their ears to teach them to hear with their eyes too! Shakespeare, through Lear: "A man may see how this world goes with no eyes. Look with thine ears: see how// Yond justice rails upon yond simple thief. Hark, in// Thine ear: change places, and, handy-dandy, which// is the justice, which is the thief? Thou hast seen a// farmer's dog bark at a beggar?" (IV, vi, 148 – 154)

Gilles Deleuze, in a very accurate and brilliant passage, explains this link between sight, (h)earing and language:

Si la fonction de la *vue* consiste à doubler, dédoubler, multiplier, celle de l'*oreille* consiste à résonner, faire résonner. [...] Apparaît alors le rapport essentiel, la complicité de la vue avec la parole. Si la vue est perverse, la parole aussi. Car, évidemment, il ne s'agit pas, comme un enfant, de parler aux doubles et aux simulacres. Il s'agit d'en parler. [...] Tantôt la vue induit la parole, et tantôt la parole induit la vue. Mais toujours il y a la multiplicité et la réflexion de ce qui est vu et de ce qui est parlé, et aussi de celui qui voit et qui parle: celui qui parle participe à la grande dissolution des mots, et même la commande ou la provoque. (Deleuze, *Logique* 329 – 330)

The ear is the most tendered and most open organ, the one that, as Freud tells us, the infant cannot close. It is also an organ that can make you cripple and disabled, and could even turn out to be a mouth. In *King Lear*, Shakespeare seems to pose the problem of the whole play in terms of relation between the person who signs or reads, and the person who reads or (h)ears. What is essentially in question in this play is Lear's name: a spiral or curved name; and what is piercing or penetrating about it, is that there is no rapprochement to be made between the syllable that compose his name and his civil status. Writes Gilles Deleuze:

Dès qu'on nomme, dès qu'on désigne quelque chose ou quelqu'un, à condition de le faire avec la précision et surtout le style nécessaires, on le dénonce aussi: on ôte le nom, ou plutôt on fait surgir sous le nom la multiplicité du dénommé, on dédouble, on réfléchit la chose, on donne sous le même mot beaucoup de choses à voir, comme voir donne en un regard beaucoup de choses à parler. On parle jamais à quelqu'un, on parle de quelqu'un à une puissance apte à le réfléchir et à le dédoubler; par là même on ne le nomme pas sans le dénoncer à un esprit comme étrange miroir. [...] Catégories de langage: évocation, provocation, révocation. (Deleuze, *Logique* 330)

If Lear seems to live on first impressions, hearsay, the immediacy of language, it is because he has a serious hearing problem. Hearing means here judgement or what the French call "entendement." Consequently, Lear is never alerted to the underlying meaning of words. The problem of understanding is linked to that of hearing. Writes Derrida:

We know that the membrane of the tympanum, a thin and transparent partition separating the auditory canal from the middle of the ear (the cavity), is stretched obliquely. Obliquely from above to below, from outside to inside, and from the back to the front. Therefore it is not perpendicular to the axis of the canal. One of the effects of this obliqueness is to increase the surface of the impression and hence the capacity of vibration. It has been observed, particularly in birds, that the precision of hearing is in direct proportion to the obliqueness of the tympanum. The tympanum squints. (Derrida, *Margins* XIV–XV)

To squint has linguistic connections to the word leer. We could say then, that Lear's tympanum leers. Not only does Lear's tympanum leer, but Lear has a squinted and leering gaze upon reality. He seems to have no appeal to the sense of hearing. How then could he organise his discourse, if it is woven in such a way that the outside is never the outside, and that its logic is reasoned from within the vault of "otos"? Is there any margin to do this? Can we trust the hollow of an ear, the limit of Lear's tympanum that squints and vibrates? Shall we cry for the lack of hearing, the lack of organs in Lear? His tympanum, his vestibular canal, his "sheal'd peascod"? Can we rely on a discourse lacking the organ of balance and equilibrium?

King Lear offers countless examples of this kind of performative language, of what will be later termed enactment, in which the normal linguistic relations between signifier and signified, sound and sense, form and meaning are altered in those figures of disorder, as a way of opening a link from language to nature. As a matter of fact, the elements of nature do take part in the constitution of all the imagery in Lear's speech, and are the means by which he expresses his refusal and condemnation of others. In the first Act of the play Lear curses Goneril and asks Nature to make her barren: "LEAR: Hear Nature, hear! dear Goddess hear!// Dry up in her the organs of increase// And from her derogate body never spring// A babe to honour her." (I, iv, 273–276)

From Act II, Nature becomes Lear's main interlocutor and the forces of Nature are real acting characters: "LEAR: Blow, winds, and crack your cheeks! rage! Blow// Your cataracts and hurricanoes, spout// Till you have drench'd our steeples, drown'd the cocks!// You sulph'rous and thought-executing fires,// Vaunt-couriers of oak-cleaving thunderbolts,// Singe my white head! And thou, all-shaking thunder,// Streike flat the thick rotundity o'th'world!// Crack Nature's moulds, all germens spill at once// That makes ingrateful man!" (III, ii, 1 – 9)

What is to be stressed in this relationship between Lear and Nature is the notion of tragicality, based on this fusion of the power of Nature with the innermost depth of Lear the man, in such a way that they are one at the moment of wrath. Shakespeare's genius consists in showing that this apparent total fusion into one, is also purged by their total separation. Lear calls on Nature, but it does not heed his call. Even Nature seems to be a silent backdrop to Lear's woes. Lear views life from the cosmic perspective of Nature and his consciousness is presented to us as emanating from the rhythms of nature: "This tempest will not give me leave to ponder// On things would hurt me more." Nature has a view, a voice, and Lear is experiencing this inner voice. But it is a voice that does not speak. Says Jean-Jacques Rousseau of the representation of nature: "Whatever one does, noise alone does not speak to the spirit at all. The objects of which one speaks must be understood. In all imitation, some form of discourse must substitute for the voice of nature. The musician who represents noise by noise deceives himself." (Rousseau 58)

Lear's inner world is reduced to the outer world, indeed regarded in principle as one and the same thing. Considered in this way, character and nature/fate, far from being theoretically distinct, do coincide. The laws of nature seem to be elevated here to measure the character Lear. But it is not in law that things are measured here; they are measured in tragedy, where the word remains unheard, speechless. What could nature say to this gazing subject who is a viewer, but not a reader? Nature becomes only the site of projection, the guilt context of the living Lear. It corresponds to his natural condition. Nature, however is mute. But this muteness can become bliss, only of lower degree. Speechlessness: that is "the great sorrow of nature," says the Arab philosopher Ibn Arabi. Nature, because it is mute, mourns and laments language itself. Lament, just as in the case of Lear, is the most undifferentiated, impotent expression of language. This means that the essence of nature is sadness, and this makes it mute. Lear fuses with nature: all that mourns feels itself thoroughly known by the unknowable. There is, in the relation of Lear's language to nature, something that can be approximately described as over-naming: a deep linguistic reason for all melancholy and all muteness.

These considerations leave us a purified concept of language: man communicates through name, which he gives to nature. Nature becomes a secret password that allows man to enter language, navigating through the multiple layers of signification, reading what was never written. Consequently, nature becomes for Lear that force which can efface all the unpleasant inconsistencies of our literate civilisation; it can show and name; it can shape and say; it can reproduce and articulate; it can imitate and signify; it can look and read. But in presenting multiple voices and in exploring the obscurity of human relationships and the fragmenting effect of the division of the kingdom, Shakespeare shows the force of cultural disruption in linguistic and aesthetic interruptions. It is under such a perspective that the patterns of sound and silence are presented as counterbalancing and unifying psychological and cultural forces. Shakespeare draws our attention to the fact that language is always saying less about situations than the sum of these same situations, and the experiences of the characters. Characters are always surrounded by the silence of the incommunicable. These Lines of poetry, voiced and unvoiced, these sounds and words of meaning, this art of the play, all grow out of the silent stirrings of the mind. Somehow, language in *King Lear* is nothing else but a "sous-rature," as Derrida might claim: words split, syllables divide, sounds disappear in order to reappear, words are rubbed out and again reformed as soon as they are spoken. Obviously, if words do not seem to work anymore, the only appreciation of language is to be found in silence, in the margin, in the limit and "the double bind," in the obscure, and in madness. Language becomes a source of frustration, rather than of expression, and non-communication seems to be the norm. "Blow, crack, spout, thunder, strike, spill, fire": words related to sound, fury, and curse! Hasn't Roman Jakobson called our attention to onomatopoeia as one of the chief poetic devices, through which sound approximates sense, and that it represents a classic example of the kind of language, in which the differences between sign and referent that characterise language as a system, are apparently foreclosed from the side of the phonetic signifier, much as they are by metaphor and its variants from the side of the semantic signified? As a last resort, Lear will try by all means to banish the invincible absence that defeats words, imposing upon them the visible form of their referent, attempting to escape the flight of circumstances, and the falling of the rain. He will recreate everything with recollections: here, recollections turn toward the future, not the past; it is the promise of an end, the end of Lear, which is in fact a re-beginning. Lear's madness could be accounted for as an excess of remembrance; a memory without a referent, a memory not of what is external, some event or fact, but of what is internal, a desire, a reminiscence. We recognise here what is at stake in any confession: the possibility of unveiling a subjective identity, a project that entails both sincerity and expressiveness: "LEAR: Didst thou give all to thy daughters?// And art thou come to this?" (III, iv, 48 – 49)

To express oneself in such a situation is an impossible task for one cannot press words hard enough to extract the nectar from their inner heart or mind. Lear's language – though judged inadequate as self expression – retains, nonetheless, a certain power: that of naming, and through naming, a mastering of the object. Every character in the play names, or judges him, categorising him as mad. But Lear can claim the power of mastery inherent in words as well; he too can name, and categorise:

> LEAR: How now, daughter! what makes that frontlet
> on? You are too much of late i'th'frown. (I, iv, 186 – 187)

> LEAR: I would learn that; for by the marks of sovereignty,
> Knowledge, and reason, I should be false persuaded
> I had daughters. (I, iv, 229 – 231)

> LEAR: The King would speak with Cornwall; the dear father
> Would with his daughter speak, commands, tends service:
> Are they inform'd of this? My breath and blood! (II, iv, 98 –
> 100)

> LEAR: You must bear with me.
> Pray you now, forget and forgive: I am old and foolish. (I, vii,
> 83 – 84)

To say "I am foolish" is already logically a contradiction in terms: either Lear is mad, and what he says is nonsense, or else, he is saying something meaningful, and is therefore sane (at least at the moment of saying it). Lear contradicts himself as he speaks, problematising the statements he issues. The question that arises is: Who is mad in the text? Who is thinking in the text? Can we suggest aphoristically that not all who would go mad, do go mad? So it is this very madness that the reader must rigorously place in doubt. If there is madness in the text, – and that can be maintained – it is not where the writer thinks he sees it. It does not lie in the thematic meaning, but somewhere else. This madness is a name for its being other, a difference from the world. It is the world around Lear that seems to be mad and Lear is nothing but a page of this world of dementia. Being mad means here being different, a mode of being different, of being other, a seemingly negative self-definition that is actually positive. Negation is here a structural concept of reflection, an index of determining thought, characteristic of the sphere of judgment. It is also a methodical tool of reflection, and it belongs also to the sphere of cognition, a sphere of pure positing thought. Madness is not an assertion of a fact, but the locus of an aspiration, the desire for madness, a blind rush toward meaning, a hyperbole of the self produced through an intoxication of language. In other reasonable terms, we would say that the truth of the world and the truth of reason do not at any rate lie within the boring dialectic of reason, but in the void of the work of art in which reason and the world must answer the threat and the question of nothingness. By the madness which interrupts it, a work of art opens a void, a moment of silence, a question without an answer; it provokes a breach without reconciliation, where the world/word is forced to question itself. It is the contestation of madness that leads the world to question itself in terms of its restoration and being: "O! matter and impertinency mix'd;// Reason in madnes."

In his final agony and analysis of events, Lear resorts to the metaphor of the looking-glass: "LEAR: Howl, howl, howl! O! you are men of stones// Had I your tongues and eyes, I'd use them so// That heaven's vault should crack. She's gone for ever// I know when one is dead, and when one lives;// She's dead as earth. Lend me a looking-glass;// If that her breath will mist or stain the stone,// Why, then she live." (V, iii, 256 – 262)

Here, we are at the end of the play and see Lear enter with Cordelia dead in his arms. It is on this very stage that Lear has very obviously outrun the limits of verbal communication. He could be depicted as a man who has lost all the linguistic forms appropriate to such a situation. His "Howl, howl, howl" is a non verbalised cry: Lear at this point is looking beyond language for evidence of life. Cordelia's inert body serves to emphasise her particular involvement with silence, her belonging to that sphere of the non verbal, and her intimate relationship with "Nothing" that has marked her from the beginning of the play. Lear seems even to grasp that Cordelia's "Nothing" might urgently communicate. There is a shift from "Nothing" to "Noting". Such "Noting" might even become the basis for creating something out of nothing. Writes David Willbern:

> From her voiced "Nothing" to her mute voice as "an excellent thing," Cordelia's discourse traces a circle of absent presence. She is the queen of silence, reciprocating Lear's tragic stature as the king – "every inch"– of nothing (Hamlet: "The king is a thing ... of nothing" [IV, ii, 28 – 30]). *Rex* becomes *res* becomes *rien*. Or in the uncanny wisdom of Lear's Fool, "uncle" is "nuncle" (*none*-cle): "Can you make no use of nothing, nuncle?" (I, iv, 130). Cordelia's nothing, at beginning and end, circumscribes or pinpoints the elemental absence of the center of Lear's world. She is, to use Kent's phrase, "the true blank of [his] eye (I, i, 159). Her silence and absence describe the center of the target of his sight; and the "blank" (target center) is blank (empty, nothing). Lear's banishment of Cordelia shuts out a symbolic vision he cannot bear to see. "We / Have no such daughter," he says to France, "nor shall ever see/ That face of hers again" (I, i, 262 – 64). Its features remind him of nothing (the "face between her forks"). Eventually he will meet its most traumatic mask, represented by Gloucester's bloody eyeless face, into whose vacancy he stares as he delivers his "down from the waist" diatribe. (Willbern 128)

The image of the "looking glass" could be the place where vision reflects itself, discovering in itself the centre and the measure of all images, perceived, imitated and invented. But it seems that such an activity of synthesis and unification is forbidden to Lear's vision, which can no longer reflect itself, because in order that his eyes see, they need another gaze. The "looking glass" image is a sign of an enigmatic and confused comprehension. If the eye is a looking glass, this means that there is no opposition between the finite and the infinite, between the visible and the invisible. This approach could be deconstructed: in order that the exterior world exist, it is necessary that we have a representation of it; this is the reason why our thought must be like a mirror where the images of the real are formed. The mirror is therefore a way of questioning the individual, not in the abstract, but in the space of the concrete. Moreover, the mirror reflection can be seen as the analogical model of a philosophical thought or reflection, because it shows the distance of the self to the self, the splitting of the thought with itself. Certainly no one likes to see himself as a stranger in a mirror, where what he sees is not his own double, but someone whom he would have liked to have been.

According to Paul de Man, for example, the self reflecting mirror effect, by means of which a work of fiction asserts its separation from empirical reality, characterises the work of literature in its essence. The "looking glass" image can be considered here as a natural mediation, and the eye mirror as the pole of a reciprocal relationship that preserves thought against the risk of losing itself in a reflection that comes back over and over again. Agnès Minazzoli was unquestionably right in admitting that:

Si le miroir est un modèle de référence susceptible de représenter l'activité psychique, il est aussi un instrument pour la pensée qui cherche à discerner le sens de ses propres actes de perception, de ses mouvements de réflexion et de connaissance. Certes, on peut affirmer que la pensée est comme un miroir, mais l'analogie n'a pas de signification si l'on ignore l'usage du miroir... Si l'esprit devient possesseur de ce qu'il réfléchit, le miroir est-il un modèle d'ordre, de pouvoir et de législation? On consulte un miroir, on l'interroge, on lui délègue le pouvoir de décider pour nous de l'exactitude, de la justesse, de la beauté de ce qu'il reflète, et ainsi progressivement en vient-on, comme dans les contes, à personnifier ce miroir à la réponse aussi attendue que redoutée, vestige, dans notre héritage culturel, de la magie catoptrique... Dans sa neutralité, le miroir tient lieu d'arbitre, et peut représenter le regard du "dehors", le regard extérieur. (Minazzoli 99)

For Jacques Lacan, the mirror (stage) is a psychological moment in which the human infant, before it has achieved the ability to coordinate and control its bodily energies and impulses, achieves an apprehension of control and unity by identifying with a totalising image of itself which comes from itself. (See Lacan, *Ecrits* 89–97) As a matter of fact, Lacan stresses the incommensurable relation between the totalising image seen in the mirror and the relatively uncoordinated state of the body which would assume and embrace that vision of totality. As a consequence of this incommensurability, the ego is from the first marked by an unbridgeable gap, a fundamental otherness or alienation, since it is constituted as an ideality which is as unattainable – or imaginary – as it is fiercely, narcissistically desired. Is it the case here to say that Lear's request for a "looking glass" is a regression in age, since the mirror phase, according to Lacan, occurs in the human individual between the ages of six months and eighteen, a period at which despite his imperfect control over his own bodily activities, "le petit homme" is first able to imagine himself as a coherent and self governing entity? Lacan's concept of the mirror phase reaches far beyond the confines of child psychology for its fullest validation. Towards the end of the passage a theory of language and a theory of interpersonal perception are taking shape; another order of experience is emerging over and against the order of imaginary identifications which the specular moments inaugurates.

We may perhaps read the use of the image of "looking glass" in linguistic terms: the image of the totalised, coherent, visionary self gazed at in the mirror becomes the signified for the relatively incoherent collection of energies, impulses, signifiers which move through the body of Lear, the "gazer." Lear's "Lend me a looking-glass," sends us back again to the problem of perception and knowledge. The mirror is here an instrument of decision; it is the referee, and it represents the exterior gaze par excellence. The spirit is an eye, the eye a mirror, and the mirror a good judge. It is an instrument of verification, ascertaining and auditing. The mirror represents also, and above all, the flight of time, the precariousness of appearances, the nearing of death: it is related to the figure of death, it contains it and reflects its image. And here, and since the ego is another, the eye seeing its "I" (seeing itself) sees something other than itself. This otherness threatens that "I" (eye), its bliss and unity. So the common element in all this, is the lack of a self sameness of subject and self representation that would enable Lear a full self knowledge. The subject, or self, or agent, cannot directly know himself as subject, but only as object or, in grammatical terms, as complement. That Lear sees a reflection and not himself in the mirror, indicates tacitly that seeing does not count as self cognition, or at least not enough to make a difference. This reflection, structuring a difference that does not count as one, is a mere fabrication, a redaction of the mirror stage, but from an adult perspective, an adult – Lear – who is behaving like a child. Shall we venture to say here that this phase of "looking glass" represents this tendency of Lear to seek and foster the imaginary wholeness of an ideal ego? This unity invented at these moments, and this ego that is the product of successive inventions, are both attempts to find ways round certain inescapable factors of lack, absence and incompleteness in human living. Lear's reality is a chaos upon which language operates. His real is created, invented and structured only for himself; it cannot be named, and hence it becomes the irremediable and intractable outside of language, and, paradoxically, may serve both to reintroduce problems and asymmetries into what could easily have become a facile dualism between the symbolic and the imaginary. About this mirror-stage and the function of the "I", Lacan writes:

Il suffit de comprendre le stade du miroir comme une *identification* au sens plein que l'analyse donne à ce terme: à savoir la transformation produite chez le sujet quand il assume une image, — dont la prédestination à cet effet de phase est suffisamment indiquée par l'usage, dans la théorie, du terme d'*imago*. [...]. C'est que la forme totale du corps par quoi le sujet devance dans un mirage la maturation de sa puissance, ne lui est donnée que comme *Gestalt*, c'est-à-dire dans une extériorité où certes cette forme est-elle plus constituante que constituée mais où surtout elle lui apparaît dans un relief de stature qui la fige et sous une symétrie qui l'inverse, en opposition à la turbulence de mouvements dont il s'éprouve l'animer. Ainsi cette *Gestalt* dont la prégnance doit être considérée comme liée à l'espèce, bien que son style moteur soit encore méconnaissable, – par ces deux aspects de son apparition symbolise la permanence mentale du *je* en même temps qu'elle préfigure sa destination aliénante; elle est grosse encore des correspondances qui unissent le *je* à la statue où l'homme se projette comme aux fantômes qui le dominent, à l'automate enfin où dans un rapport ambigu tend à s'achever le monde de sa fabrication. (4)

Isn't the mirror also and at the same time an order and a void, an order that creates void, a void that makes order between what belongs to the body and what belongs to the soul, between what imprisons and what releases, between the perishable and the immortal? It is an abyss, a grave of regrets: "LEAR: A plague upon you, murders, traitors all!// I might have sav'd her; now she's gone for ever!// Cordelia, Cordelia! stay a little. Ha!" (V, iii, 268 – 270)

If the "looking glass" is a voice of wisdom, it tells us that nothing lasts, that "All friends shall taste// the wages of their virtue, and all foes// The cup of their deservings," and that "Men must endure// Their going hence, even as their coming hither:// Ripeness is all."

It would be relevant to provide here some considerations that may help us understand the relationship between sight and knowledge in Western thought, in order to situate Shakespeare, and the ocular or anti ocular discourse, which prevails throughout his tragedy of *King Lear*. The first and most obvious consideration worth mentioning is that nobody would deny that traditionally, sight enjoys a privileged role as the most discriminating and trustworthy of the sensual mediators between man and his world. Vision has been accorded a special role in Western epistemology since the Greeks. The visual contribution to knowledge has been credited with far more importance than that of any other sense. Just think about common words and phrases in English, such as, insight, perspective, overview, far sighted, survey, point of view, demonstration, vision, look, gaze, and many others, to realise that everything seems to be oriented towards sight –"if you see what I mean!" Who more than Shakespeare, Descartes, Carlyle, Rousseau, Merleau-Ponty, Baudelaire, Valéry, and many others, have emphasised the mental representations in the mind's eye as mirror reflections of an external reality? Those spiritual optics, the sun, the moon, the stars, fire, mirrors, looking glasses, day and night, are essential ingredients in Shakespeare's writing. They show these intimate and complicated linkages between vision and psychological phenomena. *King Lear*, for example, could be read as an obsession with sight and vision, and it shows in full this fundamental relationship between ocular experience and desire, especially in its unfulfilled form. The visual domination and the discourse of sight is tremendously strong in this play. This implies that Shakespeare recognises important links between sight, knowledge and power. Maybe, behind all these mysteries, Shakespeare's intention is to show that an embodied vision, that includes the reversible, the interwining of the visible and the invisible, the viewer and the viewed, the known and the unknown, could be the locus of positive meanings. Otherwise, there would always be a split between the subject and the object of his sight: "See better Lear," recommended Kent.

It is incredibly striking that Shakespeare condemns sight in such a way as to let the eyes of Gloucester be gouged. Is this Shakespeare's last and final perception of vision and perspective? Is Shakespeare against the ontology of vision? Is this a manifestation of an anti-visual discourse? Why this emphasis on the sinister implications of sight, in for example, "Your eyes in a heavy case: Yet you see how this world goes."? Is this only a privilege given to that self referentiality of language? It seems that Shakespeare's approach to the problem of sight and vision is aimed at redoubling the mask over the face, thus revealing infinite reflections of mirrors without privileging any point of originality. The blindness of sight, the opacity of the seemingly apparent, suggests the limits of linguistic meaningfulness.

The squinting vision, the upturned eye, Lear's squinting look, all this, has no meaning in Shakespeare's language, and may have no meaning since it marks the limit. Instead, it shows, or, more precisely it signals, the point at which language explodes in tears, blood, sacrifice and horror. This leads us to admit that truth and knowledge are to be sought in evident and distinct perception, not easily translatable or decipherable to the naked eye. This also means that man functions both as a metasubject of knowledge and as its proper object, viewed from afar. Nothing in man – not even his body – is sufficiently stable to serve as the basis of self recognition, or for understanding other men. Shakespeare, after all, helped to articulate the kind of complexity these relations actually embody. And while acknowledging that self knowledge remains ever partial and incomplete, he also limits the reader's epistemological basis by consistently withholding the means for a more clear sighted analysis, marking out no-go areas and arbitrarity fixed boundaries.

The structure of the play, with all its enunciations, statements, utterances, discourses, archives, ruins and monuments, seems to be contradicted by its internal logic. The basic geometry of Lear's revelation in dividing the kingdom reverses the triangle of time and the space of temporality. By a complete revolutionary revelation, the near becomes the distant, as if only in the outer windings of this chaotic and upside down atmosphere, Lear can play the guide, transforming what is revealed into an enigma. But right from the beginning of the play, we feel that there is something confined through this strange form of the secret sharing, that death would preserve and make known. So, no matter what is understandable in Lear's language, he still speaks to us from a threshold where access is inseparable from what constitutes its barrier access and barrier, in themselves equivocal, since in this indecipherable act, the question remains, to what end? What purpose? Is it only a question of that "dark purpose," uttered by Lear in the opening scene of the play? Is this done to release this death, so long dreaded, and now suddenly desired, after the sharing of the kingdom, and the loss of Cordelia? Or perhaps to discover anew this life from which Lear irresponsibly attempted to free himself, but which he had also long dreamed of prolonging through the mad act of remaining in power, though bereft of the titles of King? Is there any other key, apart from the one in the text, that could account for Lear's decision? Why create all this doubt and disseminate it by an omission? How to cope with all these marvels, this muffled phonetic explosion of arbitrary sentences uttered by Lear? Doesn't this self containment disconnect language from all contact, induction, deduction, seduction, and thus become a mere surreptitious communication? A communication that promises nothing, made of words which are both different and the same? The whole network of words and signs issues marvellously from the tenuousness of meaning, which, sent into two different directions, is suddenly brought face to face with itself, and hence, forced to meet again. The dialogue between Lear and Cordelia is an illustrative example: Cordelia's "Nothing" has nothing to do with Lear's use of "Nothing." The identity of words – the simple and fundamental fact of language that there are fewer terms of designation than there are thoughts to designate – is itself a two sided experience. It reveals words as the unexpected meeting place of thought and spoken language. This shows again the duality of language which starts from a single core, divides itself in two and produces new figures. In their wealth of poverty, words always refer away from and lead back to themselves; they are lost and found again; they fix a vanishing point on the horizon, by repeated division, and then return to the starting point, in a perfect curve. The double meaning of word is like the image of a mask on top of a face. Regan and Goneril belong to this duality, this concealed speech that hides its real intentions, and manipulates understanding. We know the circle of language that connects the same word to different meanings. Close to it is the circle of time. In this way, the first statement of Lear – "dark purpose" – appears as an enigma. At this point, language functions as if it were denying all meanings: the eruption of things into view without horizon, the disorientation, the absence of all reference or proportion, the immobilisation of meaning. A tragic and clear present for Lear who is negotiating his power and sovereignty!

King Lear is a play dramatically structured as a dynamic system of excess and lack, metaphorically represented in a polarity of self and other that engenders, in its turn a chain of polarities: inside/outside, life/death, hiding/revealing, eye/ear, reason/madness. All the experience of the real and the unreal passes through language, and is lived with the consciousness that tells and narrates the world: things are less than words. Words have the qualities and the mystery of things. It is language itself that represents the Other. At the centre of *King Lear* there is a deliberate gap, an abyss, a sort of cosmological emptiness into which we are thrown. A sensitive analysis, reading, study of this tragedy gives us a sense of having been thrown outward and downward until we are left beyond values, altogether bereft. Maybe Heidegger was right in insisting that what he called "throwness" belongs together with projection. Shakespeare excels in this cognitive acuity, this linguistic energy, and this power of imagination. William Carlos Williams, one of the most daring and appreciative readers of Shakespeare's language, poetry and imagination, writes:

In description words adhere to certain objects, and have the effect on the sense of oysters, or barnacles. But the imagination is wrongly understood when it is supposed to be a removal from reality in the sense of John of Gaunt's speech in Richard the Second: to imagine possession of that which is lost. It is rightly understood when John of Gaunt's words are related not to their sense as objects adherent to his son's welfare or otherwise but as a dance over the body of his condition accurately accompanying it. By this means of the understanding, the play written to be understood as a play, the author and reader are liberated to pirouette with the words which have sprung from the old facts of history, reunited in present passion. To understand the words as so liberated is to understand poetry. That they move independently when set free is the mark of their value. Imagination is not to avoid reality, nor is it description nor an evocation of objects or situations, it is to say that poetry does not tamper with the world but moves it — It affirms reality most powerfully and therefore, since reality needs no personal support but exists free from human action, as proven by science in the indestructibility of matter and of force, it creates a new object, a play, a dance which is not a mirror up to nature but — As birds' wings beat the solid air without which none could fly so words freed by the imagination affirm reality by their flight. (Williams 234)

Shakespeare's writing reflects in full this power to originate, and this gift in evidencing a psychology of mutability. Shakespeare is the originator of the depiction of self change on the basis of self overhearing. There is always in him this difference in kind and in degree which shows that his characters always appear infinite. They are always open to a multitude of perspectives, and can become analytical instruments for judging the reader. Writes Harold Bloom: "If you are a moralist, Falstaff outrages you; if you are rancid, Rosalind exposes you; if you are dogmatic, Hamlet evades you forever. And if you are an explainer, the great Shakespearean villains will cause you to despair. [...] The most bewildering of Shakespearean achievements is to have suggested more contexts for explaining us than we are capable of supplying for explaining his characters. Shakespeare's uncanny ability to present consistent and different actual-seeming voices of imaginary beings stems in part from the most abundant sense of reality ever to invade literature." (Bloom, *The Western* 65)

In addition to that function of imaginative writing, Shakespeare teaches us a prevailing and dominant lesson of poetry: how to speak to others, but more importantly, how to speak to ourselves. Nature is presented in two contrasting views: the traditional view of Bacon, which assumes that nature is rational and divinely ordered, and the view of the rationalists that man is governed by appetite and self interest. Certainly, Shakespeare was fully aware of the two conceptions of nature in his times, for he would have found them in Montaigne (5) or in Sidney. (6) But Montaigne, who "peignait non l'être mais le passage" seems to have influenced Shakespeare more than any other philosopher. As a matter of fact, both Montaigne and Shakespeare could be located in this thought tour where all contradictions are unresolved, where everything has a wrong side or a reverse, and where every light creates a shadow. Comedy has a hidden sadness, tragedy an exhilarating grandeur. Madness and lucidity go hand in hand against the spirit of seriousness and despair, with all the paradoxes stated by Erasmus. Tragedy is burlesque, comedy is sad, and Molière himself will be inclined to the natural. The world is comic to thought, but tragic to sensitivity.

These experiences, visible, sensitive, have already been dealt with, but they are always represented. What is to be noted is that Shakespeare violates those accepted rules of taste which had been established by French classicism. He discredits the concept of poetic rules, and even the idea of poetic artifice. In his work as a whole, nature is seen through clashing perspectives: Lear and Edmund, Hamlet and Claudius, Othello and Iago. What seems to matter is the mutilation of nature, and our sense of what is natural or unnatural in our lives. The effect is so overwhelming and misleading that, at *King Lear*'s close, everything seems to have turned against itself. We are strongly affected by Lear's death, yet we do not know why. Maybe we lack that insight into the Shakespearean representation of character, that still needs to be developed. Maybe we are far from understanding that detachment, typical of Shakespeare, that helps create an art of exclusion. We cannot give any explanation of the fact that Shakespeare remembers certain details as he describes each individual, while forgetting, excluding, or even censoring others. The magnificence of Shakespeare lies in his power of representation of the human character and personality, and their mutabilities. One could say, that Shakespeare infuses in us an energy, a high power that helps to go back to the future, and to prefigure a past which clarifies needs still to enjoy in full! There is a sort of individuation of speech, an appropriateness of speech to character; an art of division, differentiating and creating differences. Establishing a standard for measuring representation, Shakespeare marks, remarks, traces, presents, represents and shadows in full prospect. He has this power of changing cognition by changing the representation of cognition. The play as a text, relinquishes its status as identity, and affirms its condition as pure difference. In other words, the text redefines itself, inscribes itself in a texture or network of meanings which are not limited to the text itself. With Shakespeare, we go to the concrete universal (the universal conditions of human existence), and in details, we see for a fact diversity, the ways of living, temperaments. We are therefore in nature, as it is given, and in all its details, as a luxuriant diversity.

On the contrary, our modern world is dominated by culture and history: Hobbes, Rousseau, Kant. They go from the solitary individual, supposed to be the most concrete reality. We, moderns or post-moderns, hope for unification, surpassing, but humanity is never punctual, and the result, despite the will effort, is imperfect. It is of little importance if "les Modernes" are inferior or superior to "les Anciens"; their reform/enterprise of nature seems, in every case, to impregnate them with disappointment and throw them in solitude and suspicion. Against these modern generalisations, Shakespeare shows that love and friendship between beings resist all forms of generalisation, and that morality is not opposed to pleasure. Says Gil Delannoi: "C'est en mathématique que l'esprit trouve la plus grande généralité; l'identité de pensée est absolue dans une démonstration refaite séparément par deux esprits. La poésie, à l'extrême opposé, est heureusement transmissible, par sympathie, mais ne recouvre jamais deux expériences identiques. On ne lit jamais deux fois le même poème. On n'a jamais vécu deux amours strictement identiques. Cet universel-là passe obligatoirement par la particularité de l'expérience, mais cette particularité n'est compréhensible, transmissible, communicable que par référence à l'universel. Alors, *diversité et naturel* sont les alliés de l'humanité." (Delannoi 56)

Hamlet may give the answer to this:

Be not too tame neither, but let your own discretion be your tutor: suit the action to the word, the word to the action, with this special observance, that you o'erstep not the modesty of nature; for anything so overdone is from the purpose of playing, whose end, both at the first and now, was and is, to hold, as't were, the mirror up to nature; to show virtue her own feature, scorn her own image, and the very age and body of the time his form and pressure. Now, this overdone, or come tardy off, though it make the unskilful laugh, cannot but make the judicious grieve; the censure of which one must in your allowance o'erweigh a whole theatre of others. (III, ii, 19–33)

What is most remarkable in Shakespeare is this craving for diversity, and this mixture of styles. Shakespeare has attained a certain "non-moi" that is so particular, yet so universal. It is in this sense that Harold Bloom, on his meditation on love and friendship, (Bloom, *L'Amour*) understands the genius and the universality of Shakespeare. For Bloom, Shakespeare should be read, seen, heard in the concrete universality, in the fact that men are born and die, take pleasure and suffer, love and hate. It is precisely this confounding natural state that Bloom calls a miracle of conformity with Nature. The best way to feel diversity is to perceive it as the infinite detail of the concrete universal. This latter can only be a nature. It is this diversity that gives Shakespeare his inimitable naturalness. All the characters seem to speak like Shakespeare, and not a single character speaks in the same way. Even personality in our sense, is a Shakespearean invention, and it is not only Shakespeare's greatest originality but also the authentic cause of his perpetual pervasiveness, as Harold Bloom opines in his outrageously ambitious *Shakespeare: The Invention of the Human*. A titanic claim, that of Bloom, who makes us wonder whether Shakespeare's influence on the whole of our lives might not be simply the sober truth.

Having Bloom in mind and without swallowing his argument whole, *King Lear* may represent for us difference itself; its textuality is in its differing from itself. We cannot determine once and for all, which meaning or meanings, which interpretation or interpretations, which reading or readings prevail, and which do not. There is in this play a double bind that refuses to see, and it is rampant throughout the whole play of *King Lear*. It could be a perverted desire that does not speak of itself. Shakespeare's discourse, in general, does not have an overwhelming interest in certainty,

literal truth, or speculative coherence. It teaches us, only too well, of whatever truth we can sustain without perishing. In representing so perfectly the
uncertainty of the human condition, Shakespeare torments us. There seems
to be no energy that looks for its own reflection by reaching back on itself,
but there is instead, a transvaluational one that moves beyond itself to other
transforming configurations. The desire that generates nature for instance,
is not founded in nature. What really matters is the mutilation of nature,
and our sense of what is or is not natural in our lives. In other words, it is an
insistent interest on the part of the human organisation of forces in preserv-
ing its human difference in an otherwise un-human setting. What setting is
more un-human than that of *King Lear*? Nature functions in the service of
the human will to distinction, privilege, and domination. Shakespeare certainly believes that without order, chaos reigns; he sees the need for society
to be a microcosm of the cosmic design, a mimicry of nature, but recognises the capriciousness of nature as well as its harmony. He appears as
the playwright of that constant movement to different levels of speech, of
a systematic disengagement from the "I" who has begun to speak; a writer
who shifts in the distance, separating a speaker from his words. He measures the limit, the margin and the extremity where thought can take place.
Very often, his language develops from the dispersal; relation is as often intrusion and collusion as coherence or recognition. In this dispersion, words
are born in differences, and the totality of understanding is never apparent.
We feel that stretch of being that is beyond comprehension – the mystery
of being. We have the impression that Shakespeare's discourse disturbs and
fragments what is generally considered to be unchanging or unified. It becomes like a counter-memory. It is a challenge to accepted Order of things,
a world in which all is examined and questioned.

Lear for example, teaches us that man does not transcend either nature or time as object, but develops and behaves within them; nor does
time transcend man, the subject and the object of knowledge. Man is the
knower/known who embodies a gap that is designed to be overcome. Consequently, man occurs as a question to himself; he is the knower/known, the
subject that produces himself as a knowable object, the basis for the orders
of knowledge in which he lives and develops: "LEAR: O! reason not the
need; our basest beggars// Are in the poorest thing superfluous:// Allow not

nature more than nature needs,// Man's life is as cheap as beast's." (II, iv, 262 – 265)

King Lear also brings under scrutiny Shakespeare's perceptions of being, mind, feelings, knowledge, and language, especially that mute silent part of it. As a matter of fact, in defining silence as a meaningful presence, and not just as an absence, Shakespeare elevates language, praising silence as an enlightened presence and liberating it from the violence and unreliability of the word. He seems suspicious of actual speech. Silence has its lexicon, its punctuation, and its metaphors. Talk, which has been valued as "presence mastered", as Derrida says, is now marked as absence, lack of what is supposed to convey. Talk becomes, in this way, the uncertainty of feelings, love, and life. Words are loosened upon words. It is silence that points out language's mask: the uncertainties and limitations of interpretation. It is silence that reveals the ambiguities of language. Of course, language reveals something through words, but it conceals many other things through silence. In other words, the essence of meaning and communication is not only in language, but mainly in silence: "What shall Cordelia speak? Love, and be silent." Silence is the ground of speech, just as "Nothing" is the very ground of Being. Speech happens in silence, silence happens in speech. Silence, too, can speak; it can be, as we say, pregnant; and when silences are broken, they are also filled; they are spaces or times for talk, occasions for creation and recreation. Cordelia's "Love and be silent" could also be interpreted as a plea for a meaningful, concise use of language. Not only is love itself (Cordelia's) action enough – the word love itself contains enough meaning to preclude the use of further words.

Cordelia's silence is given a being; it is the narration of the unspoken, the real said of the unsaid. This means that though thought and speech are clearly related, the physical voice need not the metaphoric model for mind or presence. We cannot, save metaphorically, ask in words of that which lies beyond words. Certainly, there are other hidden aspects of language. The art of writing does not at all depend upon that of speaking. The Platonic view that speech is the origin of writing does not hold that much. Georges Steiner, in his *Real Presences*, urges for an exploration of the unspoken and the unvoiced:

Expelled from silence, language does its irreparable work. [...] There may indeed be such sentences in the unvoiced, inward monologue of the deaf- mute and the autistic. Writing also, offers what comes very near to being a disposal of the impossibility of the unending: in Sade's prose, punctuation marks are nothing more than a pause for breath, scornfully conceded, in a language-act which aims to exhaust, to exploit devouringly, the entirety of the sensory sets, series and combinations latent in imagining. [...] Speech can change the rules under which it operates in the course of its operation, making the green one red. (Steiner, *Real* 53 – 58)

We should distinguish, at this point, the representation of thought and the representation of speech. Speech sends us back to sound, voicing, fiction, audibility, construction and deconstruction; in a word, to the notion of risk. On the contrary, thought is related to silence, to inaudibility, and invoicing. It is a free-indirect discourse, and is most of the time not expressed in words or sounds. It is the unwritten that blurs interpretation. When the self speaks to the self, who is speaking after all? Cordelia's asides show that those who are generally silent cannot find the appropriate language registers or forms of expressions. Cordelia is acutely aware of the unsaid, and even the unthought. Doesn't Shakespeare develop more of an interest in the inner life of those on the margins of speech? Doesn't he also develop – and this is an experimental gift in theatricality – a technique, or a method of indirection for saying the unsaid, the unspeakable, and for illuminating the minds of the readers? Doesn't he seem to diffuse the semiotic and the symbolic, in summoning silence into text as language, that is to say as a presence? Silence is no more seen from a foreign land; it is not loss, it is not lack, it is not absence, it is not darkness, and it is not negation. It is something that cannot be represented, something that is not said; something above and beyond language. Consequently, Cordelia's thoughts cannot, at any rate, express themselves in words, in that repressive, utilitarian world of facts.

We, readers of the end of the twentieth century, cannot miss the suggestiveness of a word such as trace, which reminds us of the layers of language – of which Derrida speaks – and figures – which Genette describes as the gap between a sign and its meaning, the inner space of language. It is Shakespeare who presents this oppressed silence of a woman, Cordelia, who, through excess or lack of expressiveness, was misinterpreted, and misread. It is Shakespeare who stresses the principle of sufficient reason, that of "Nothing." "Nothing" is without grounds as it is normally asserted, but curiously when we stress it, it can sound wholly positive, conclusive, and self evident. When it is stressed, we tend to pass through it, to think it away, and to drop it. We seem to be thrown in a world where nothing is concluded. Nothing is concluded in the play because meaning lives on in the reader. So the paradox of reading silence, or reading the unreadable, requires a sharp attention, perhaps dormant in this play of speech and noise. Is it relevant here to say that Shakespeare is to be praised? He created a different method to represent the life of language, as experienced not in the speech, but in the consciousness of a character, inviting the reader to enter and clarify the complete text. In other words, he/she who reads should add to what is not said, in order to read it and frame or reframe it. However, Shakespeare always makes sure that we do know what is unsaid. Just because Cordelia does not say it does not mean the audience does not know it. It is therefore on this level that Shakespeare appears as an informer of a critical vision that provides a way of making silence readable. Shakespeare passionately believes that all that really matters in human life is precisely what, in his view, we must be silent about. He is a breaker of a whole mould, venturing into the field of silence, expressing the nuances of silence with a lexicon of asides, nothings, gulfs, abyss, absence, and interruption. Such views are represented and shared by Beckett, Mallarmé, Eluard, Celan, and many others. Virginia Woolf, through Bernard in *The Waves*, speaks of the fact that: "For pain words are lacking. There should be cries, cracks, fissures, whiteness passing over chintz covers, interference with the sense of time, of space; the sense also of extreme fixity in passing objects; and sounds very remote and then very close; flesh being gashed and blood spurting, a joint suddenly twisted – beneath all of which appears something very important, yet remote, to be just held in solitude." (Woolf, *The Waves* 226)

Silence becomes a concept that expresses harmony, balance, meditation and pondering. Literature becomes an open field to a new life, freeing us from the pressure of the fixed meaning of language, maintaining as long as possible an opening, an uncertainty of signs, which allow us to breathe. Silence also disturbs, because through it, literature draws attention to itself, and points out its mask. Silence is nothing but resistance, and especially resistance to interpretation. What is in fact 'seen' is not a given, objective reality open to an innocent eye. To achieve fullness of meaning, one must punctuate. Says Barbara Johnson: "A deconstructive reading is an attempt to show that the conspicuously foregrounded statements in a text are systematically related to discordant signifying elements that the text has thrown into its shadow or margins; it is an attempt both to recover what is lost and to analyse what happens when a text is read solely in fonction of intentionality, meaningfulness, and representivity." (Barbara Johnson 279)

Consequently, lexical items in the tragedy of *King Lear*, such as "nothing," "eye-sighted," "O without a figure," "peascod," do function as themes, images, markers, and symbols of an interior distance. They bring into focus the interval, the chasm, and the abyss, signaling the character's retreat from sensory immediate experience, and entrance into the world of the unsaid, the universe of silent consciousness, where the mind discovers its powers to evolve, and is not trapped in the actual, travelling thus, freely in open spaces. It is the space of Cordelia, a space with no external time; a space that cannot be situated or positioned in the external world; a space where thought can see simultaneously different relations and different aspects: "CORDELIA: Time shall unfold what plighted cunning hides;// Who covers faults, at last with shame derides. (I, i, 279 – 280)

Cordelia represents what could be called in Derridean terms, the double movement: the concentration and contradiction of self necessary for stillness of mind; that is to say, the reflection of that dynamism between inside and outside. What is seen is behind the eyes, and what is perceived has not yet been expressed. What is happening is always richer than we who try to express it. Shakespeare seems in this regard to deconstruct or outplay the codes on which he relies, or seems to: life conflicts with something that is not life: "the bond cracks between son and father," and "the mouth should tear the hand for lifting food to it." By encompassing all these voices and views, Shakespeare represents a particular tonal sense of reality. Sentences are unfinished, language does not bear anymore what it contains. These multiple views and voices fragment language and life. Speech is deconstructed, and distanced from the matter at hand; silence is introduced to slow down the heaviness and repressiveness of time, that is always "out of joint," and it becomes a part of a pattern, a space for interaction, and hence language is maximised: it is not the spoken word, but what is behind the eyes and the (h)ears. Identity and difference are established in relation to one another, not in correspondence with a true reality. There is also this incorporation of the negative shocks and conflicts of life that though, they embody the negative, they embody it in purely positive terms. So "foul is fair and fair is foul," and consequently "there is nothing good or bad, but thinking makes it so." Nothing is lost when everything is given away; in fact, everything is gained. "Nothing" means that everything that exists stands in correlation, and this correlation is the real and veritable nature of existence. In this way, the existing thing has no being of its own, but only in something else. This is to show that everything is bound to and conditioned by everything else, that no-things remain, but only dynamic quanta in relation of tension to all other dynamic quanta.

This philosophy of silence in almost all the plays of Shakespeare brings under scrutiny nothing less than the nature of mind, knowledge, and being. In redefining silence or even nothingness as a presence, and not just as an absence, Shakespeare displaces, disconnects, and disjoints the privileged place of the speaking subject, and speech or dialogue, as the only markers of presence in his plays. Silence becomes as deep as eternity, speech as shallow as time, and the learning of the grammar of silence becomes an art more difficult to learn than that of sounds. It is silence then, that is the element in which great things fashion themselves; even faint utterances of silence are agreeable to our auditory nerves; they are harmony and purest melody. Says Thoreau: "Silence is the universal refuge, the sequel to all dull discourses and all foolish acts, a balm to our every chagrin as welcome after satiety as after disappointment; that back ground which the painter may not daub, be he master or bungler, and which, however an awkward a figure we may have made in the foreground, remains ever our inviolable asylum, where no indignity can assail, no personality disturb us." (Thoreau 392)

Jacques Derrida like Shakespeare, is suspicious of the illusion of full and present speech, of the illusion of presence within a speech believed to be transparent and innocent. It is toward the praise of silence that the myth of a full presence wrenched from "différance," and from the violence of the word is then deviated. (Derrida, *Of Grammatology* 140) Would it be relevant here to state the fact that silence in the stories of *Thousand and One Nights* for instance, has its own social validity, and a real psychological effect? We are always safe if we know how to keep silent. Silence is also a frightening arm that protects those who can really know how to use it. And Arab Sufis think that silence is to know how to speak within the limit and margin of necessity; it is a trope that informs us about embarrassing or disturbing situations. Writes Malek Chebel: "Le silence est observé chaque fois qu'un personnage veut échapper à la mort. Ce fut le cas pour un jeune prince qui dut se taire pendant sept jours. [...] On peut dire, métaphoriquement, que la femme arabe est une invention du silence, qu'elle utilise savamment, car plus que la ruse que les hommes lui attribuent avec prodigalité, sa maîtrise du silence vaut largement des oppositions plus discoureuses et de franche rébellions." (Chebel 212–213)

What is to be emphasised here is that in questioning the nature of being and knowing, through the concepts of presence and absence, speech and silence, seeing and interpreting, saying and unsaying, Shakespeare is above all questioning the nature of language itself. He is looking for ways to escape language through spatialising thought and expressing the mind through the body, and all that is not related with the said or the sayable. In exploring that which is unsaid, he is exploring what happens in the hiatus between word and thing. In rupturing and breaking down the belief in the link between the word and the thing or actuality, in acknowledging silence, the ineffable, the limitations of language and interpretation, Shakespeare questions language. He seems to refuse the alphabetic signs, that servile instrument of speech, preferring instead, to restore that dignity of the non-alphabetic signs of silence. He uses words as if they were new, as if – says Steiner – "no previous touch had clouded their shimmer or muted their resonance." (Steiner, *Language* 46)

Shakespeare preaches to a reader who is able to decipher the rhetoric of silence, the language of silence; for he strongly believes that there are actions of the spirit deeply rooted in silence, and far beyond the frontiers of the spoken word. No more fragmentation and impurities engendered by syntax; reality can begin outside verbal language. He thus compels us to wonder whether reality can be spoken of, when speech is merely a kind of regression, when discourse becomes a form of trapping and fooling. This refined substance prevails in all his works, and – as Harold Bloom sustains – has proven to be multicultural, "so universally apprehended in all languages as to have established a pragmatic multiculturalism around the globe, one that already far surpasses our politicised fumblings toward such an ideal. Shakespeare is the centre of the embryo of a world canon, not Western or Eastern and less Eurocentric." (Bloom, *The Western* 63)

His drama is a real "horizon beyond which at present we do not see", as Emerson once said of Shakespeare. It is through this double fracture

that the unthinkable emerges as powerful and thinkable: repeated and inevitable disunity, lack of source, impossibility of completion and peace,
groundless anxiety, death. Shakespeare's thinking itself seems to function
here with full awareness of non human dimensions of both thinking and
speaking. How can a person think thoughts that are not his own and that are
not simple repetitions of someone's else repetitions? Can thinking in this
way be the difference between a person and a discourse? Here, everything
is based on contrasts and instantaneous effects. Contrasts of all kinds: between characters, between one decor and another, between the words of the
same character, speeches between characters. Shakespeare exploits everything; he does not necessarily choose. Unlike Racine, he seems to be for an
art of accumulation and estranged surprises to the drama. He wants by all
means – what could be called in Deleuzian terms – this "effect-affect." No
artistic elegance, only profundity and depth; very domineering indeed, and
hence very modern. Says Paul Valéry:

Shakespeare manque du bien et du besoin suprême qui est élégance. Il veut l'effet:
c'est dire que tous les moyens lui sont bons. Il spécule sur un auditeur sans défense,
ou réduit à l'impuissance par la brutalité des chocs infligés. La profondeur de
Shakespeare est un moyen de domination. Il n'est pas géomètre grec. Il ne veut pas
de la réflection sur son drame, il la repousse et la concentre sut la réalité; il attaque
donc le spectateur hors du jeu. Il est donc effroyablement moderne. Ni l'absurde,
ni le contradictoire, ni l'excessif, ni l'incohérent ne l'épouvantent. (Valéry 1185)

Shakespeare's work recalls something borne and concealed in our language: clearing, concealment, unconcealment, uncertainty, and deep puz-
zlement go together with the experience of thinking. It seems as if he had
no specific reality or realities to define or analyse. Any text in its happening
is other than what is said about it, and cannot properly be said to be either
present or absent. Breaks, ruptures, blanks, silences, dissolution, separation,
disunity are not opposed to continuity. On the contrary, these words speak
of how continuities develop and are juxtaposed with each other. Breakage
can be a part of an entire object, just as a break can happen as a replace-
ment. It is Cordelia who really represents the idea of break, elaborating the
idea of the whole event in the play. As a matter of fact, she represents the
measure against the phantasm of the naked reality; a reality which has no
origin, no judge, only an immediate verdict: "Let pride, which she calls

plainness, marry her." It is only language that knows that what is essential is both lost and present. Writes Derrida:

Le texte se présente alors comme le commentaire du mot absent qu'il délimite, enveloppe, sert, entoure de ses soins. Le texte se présente comme le métalangage du langage qui ne se présente pas. Mais il s'agit seulement de parade. Et celui qui vient ensuite exhiber les creux actifs de l'autre et prononcer l'imprononcé – parade encore comme métalangage -, simule la présentation, laisse des cloques ou des cloches, des colonnes d'air dans son corps, cerne, exclut encore d'autres mots, etc. L'agonie du métalangage est donc structurellement interminable. Mais comme effort et comme effet. Le métalangage est la vie du langage; il bat toujours de l'aile comme un oiseau pris dans une glu subtile. (Derrida, *Glas* 182)

In Shakespeare, the splitting of word and thing, subject and object, is very evident. Theatre in its essence is nothing but a form of expression, and words are only one of its tools, a necessary but contingent supplement, used to resolve the dichotomy of consciousness and reality. The structure of a play is that authority which allows the free play of elements around it, or more precisely, that fugitive presence absence which flows everywhere, and above all, at the margins of the written. The written reveals itself in what could be isolated in order to be inscribed. It reminds us of what we may never have known: the text is never a straight line, it is always held within, and constantly goes beyond its representation. The first reading of any Shakespearean play is a manifold experience: to the first experience of the narrative journey, others follow, be they in the text or on the stage, all of them oriented to assimilate the experience and the consciousness of the play, to such an extent that these same experiences become different aspects of the same thing. We must point out on the other hand, that the unification of consciousness and experience depends on the written text, which remains invariable, in order to be consulted. So, the task of the reader should aim at a certain relationship, unperceived by the writer, between what he commands and what he does not command of the patterns of language that he uses. In this way, reading becomes text-production. In *King Lear*, there is no textual fixedness whatsoever to be divined: there is that "not-seen" which limits our visibility, and which should be opened, though the "not seen" accessible to sight is always within the text and does not leave it. In other words, knowledge, true knowledge is to be sought in the blind spots. The problem is then how to induce order upon the contorted proportionless accumulation of knowledge and experience. There is in Shakespeare's writing this power of literature to resist, to divide and oppose whole meaning, to separate being from the word, or to name being as itself divides. In de Manian terms, Shakespeare's insight arises from a vision which is able to move towards blindness, only because it does not fear the power of light in blindness, and the power of blindness in light. Lear's "dark purpose" names the wavering movement of the blind Lear towards sun, light and wisdom. The fragment remains in any case a literary form; oppositions should always be brought to light, showing how power and privilege are often surreptitiously mapped onto apparently neutral oppositions, and finally dismantling or deconstructing oppositions by showing how each term shares certain attributes with its opposite, or presenting cases that the opposition cannot assimilate. The categories of language are absolute in their wrath or differentiation. The word resists language as "the grain of a tree resists the saw", and saws take the form they do partly because wood is what it is." Writes Robert Scholes:

I believe that violence and alienation are aspects of the price we pay for the textual power of language. Human beings become human through the acquisition of language, and this acquisition alienates humans from all those things that language names. The name is a substitute for the thing; it displaces the thing in the very act of naming it, so that language finally stands even between one human being and another. Much of our poetry has been written to undo this familiarity, to make the stone stoney, or, failing this, to at least make language itself visible: to make the word wordy. (Scholes 112)

Texts have always had this ambiguous power to deny and to redouble. We should perhaps approach them not to see what they reveal, but to consider what they conceal, asking the question: what violence is being done here? Interpretations are not revelations of meanings; there is never enough knowledge to account adequately for the illusion of knowing. There is always that "imperceptibility." Maybe Derrida is right when he writes in the beginning of his *Glas* that "A text is not a text unless it hides from the first comer, from the first glance, the law of its composition and the rules of its game. A text remains, moreover, forever imperceptible. Its law and its rules are not, however, harbored in the inaccessibility of a secret; it is simply that they can never be booked, in the present, into anything that could rigorously be called a perception."

If the intention and integrity of a text are invisible, this means in a certain way, that the text hides something, and therefore, it implies, states, embodies, represents, but does not immediately disclose something. The word itself is not a sign, but a "signifying knot," as Lacan says. A word is often an image of meaning as meaning, which in order to be discovered has to be unveiled. Disclosure is then dependent upon a series of powers, resident beneath textuality and knowledge. Knowledge is always in bondage, and if it gives itself as the knowledge of truth, it is because it produces truth through the play of a primary and always reconstituted falsification, which erects the distinction between truth and falsehood. As for language, it always remains a way of naming and thinking what is in essence. Heidegger for example, finds that language itself is poetry in its essential essence, and he admits that all art is, in fact, poetry, and poetry turns out to be the saying of the unconcealment of what is. (Derrida, "Plato's" 63) The status of such terms, poetry, art, and language, is typically resolved by Heidegger through a kind of reductive tautology: language is only essentially language, insofar as it is language; poetry is essentially poetry, and all of these, finally, are the same. Language, – as Heidegger seems to sustain – when it is language, at one great moment says one thing, for one time only.

Lear could be inserted in this system of language: to think of oneself, then, is to think not of oneself, but of a figure, or sign of oneself: "Thou art an O without a figure." But this "O" the sign and sound of nothing underlies speech itself. Its design underlies writing as well. The circle is found at the origin of almost all alphabets or ideograms. We could perhaps be tempted to say that Shakespeare writes against writing; he writes to make good the loss of writing, and by this very gesture forgets and denies what occurs by hand. Hence any discursive valorisation appears to be irreducibly linked to exteriority, discontinuity, alterity and delaying effect of writing. It is therefore all that is not really written that organises the various relations of speech and what is called writing. Shakespeare's "Nothing" therefore looks like "O" and sounds like an "Oh!", the basic "ejaculation" that predicts speech, the infant's Word. Our first language, as Lear reminds us, is a cry: "We came crying hither." Nothing is an infinitely meaningful phoneme, in which are rooted our most basic words about speech. Shakespeare invites us to note these vast non discursive regions that lie beyond mere words, and beyond an instrumental reason which claims to master them. There is, as a matter of fact, at the origins of the acquisition of language, of perception, of reality testing, of the capacity to symbolise or to interact creatively with an environment, a primary fact of absence, a separation and loss. Lacan, and other contemporary French psychoanalysts, emphasise this primary myth of loss in specifically linguistic terms. Lacan's "diacritical theory of meaning", for example, states that words rest finally not on anything real, but only on the circularity of mutual inter definition. It is this circularity, this "O" that makes Lacan think that meaning is "poured," and which makes Derrida say that the "signature is a wound" – and there is none other at the origin of the work of art. As Willbern maintains, the sound of "O" and its shape is also to be linked with other sounds: "No" and "Know." "No" and "Know" coalesce in the same audible syllable, harmonising the dialectical theme of knowledge and negation that *King Lear* proceeds tragically to play out and that 'Nothing' subsumes as part of its (w)hole, of its "manqué" too: "Know [. . .] that we have divided in three our kingdom." Says David Willbern:

The totality of Shakespeare's *Nothing* cannot be circumscribed by any figure of speech or design, unless it is his own wooden *O*. Shakespeare's *Nothing* is a paradox, a living world that willingly announces itself as mere bubble, words that disappear into a void. Shakespeare's theater is finally only a momentary enactment of *sight* and *sound* and *symbol,* surrounded by *silence* and a bare stage, at the last returning to where it began in emptiness and *absence*. Yet while it is there, in the playspace of *creative nothingness*, it is wondrous: beautiful or dreadful, ruinous or renascent, and uniquely *worth noting*. (Willbern 142)

Historical criticism locates Shakespeare not as some real presence, but as an absence or difference within the continuum of discourse that is our speech and writing. Shakespeare's unique authority – as Richard Wilson sustains – "derives precisely from this peculiar and primitive hermeneutic pact: that the hidden gold will manifest himself only to those who do not seek him out." (Wilson 2) How real is the signifier is the question Shakespeare constantly poses: language is something less than reality, but also its very inner form; and it is difficult to distinguish the proper from the improper. Fiction seems inherent in reality, myth and metaphor should service rather than master society; yet they are not purely supplementary to it either: they are merely disposable decor or ornaments, since they shape from within the history to which they give outward expression; society itself is a dramatic artefact, "demanding a certain suspension of disbelief," as Schoenbaum would say. But what really constitutes Shakespeare's aesthetic transcendence is his historicity that remains the big question. It is perhaps Shakespeare's own evasion of both the privileges and obligations of humanist authorship which make him so historically significant, as Marcus explains:

So far as we know, he took no particular interest in 'authoring' his plays; he did not collect and publish them himself. But there are other places where we encounter a Shakespeare every bit as captivated by the humanist enterprise as contemporaries like Ben Jonson. I am thinking in particular of the Shakespeare of the sonnets. [...] The extent to which the claims and strategies of authorship impinge on Shakespeare's drama is more variable and nearly impossible to generalize about [...] [but] if Shakespeare avoided the appearance of intentionality, it was at least part of the time by design. We must try to distinguish between a lack of intentionality and the avoidance of intentionality, which may be a radically different thing. (Marcus 40 – 41)

Shakespeare everywhere reminds us of the transformational power of words, their appearing to defy their own distinctness by overlapping and changing places with one another. "One thing expressing, leaves out difference" as he suggests in Sonnet 105. Words seem to undermine themselves and the way they are supposed to function, as if they insist on reminding us that their meanings, with oppositions flowing into one another, must be as inconstant as the experience they would record. Very often, language in effect wipes itself out as everything is made relative, contingent, arbitrary. The poet must protest a language that operates this way, though this seems to be the inevitable consequence of the function of language. Language is always – or so it appears – the locus of resistance as well as of domination; and it is this concept of discourse as a site of contest that lies behind Shakespeare's writing. At its core, *King Lear*, just like *Julius Caesar*, is a play about writing and reading, and it represents significance as the instrument of discursive power. The sharing of the kingdom could be seen as a metonym for the diaspora of language and intertextuality of writing as it circulates among the main characters of the play. Meaning itself seems forever delayed with supplementary writing, and supplement – says Derrida in *Of Grammatology* – is "another name for *différance*." Supplementarity is, as a matter of fact, the operation of differing which at once and at the same time fissures and retards presence, submitting it to primordial division and delay.

Writing about Shakespeare is challenging and pleasurable; the resource is inexhaustible, like language itself. He is the mortician of fixed meaning, the dislocator of language: those tensions and ambiguities in his meaning are the effects of the tension inherent in language itself between those two poles variously named metonymic/metaphoric, or symbolic/semiotic. His real concern was the question of whether an individual is a nonunitary sign in some larger writing, or himself a writer of signs. There is always in his writing a reference to "that within" which is never tied to a particular referentiality, but always pointing to a "somewhere else," an orphaned text, perhaps. Shakespeare has come to be an icon, an emblem, a logos, a talisman, a secular saint, a patriarch, man of the millennium. He is invariably conscripted to inflate any commonplace assertion about almost any subject from public speaking to space travel, or to provide ballast to stabilise our "rocky morale." He has been claimed for their own by Marxists, Buddhists, Catholics, Lutherans, monarchists, feminists, animists, agnostics and absurdists. He speaks across centuries, across race and class and creed. Fortunately, the fact that we know little of his life saves us from making fatuously mechanistic equations between his life and his work. He wrote thirty-nine of the best plays ever produced, and with an extraordinary fluency: "His mind and hand went together," said a contemporary. He was not a religious man. Even if God or the gods are frequently invoked, he shows no passion for organised religion. However hard one tries, one cannot conscript Shakespeare to the body of any church. The Bible is frequently quoted, explicitly and implicitly, largely because it was the only published literature available to many of his audience. And while there is an awareness in the plays of the presence of the supernatural in human affairs, doubt is always acknowledged. This is the world of the Renaissance, the age of Galileo, the age, as John Donne put it, of the "new philosophy which calls all in doubt." Shakespeare is fascinated by politics, charting the world of secular power with an avid curiosity, showing a highly developed sense of the workings of the machinery of bureaucracy and power. Students of politics who are keen to study the anatomy of opportunism, moral ambiguity, expediency and hypocrisy could take as their primer the histories and the Roman plays, and for advanced study *King Lear*, *Troilus and Cressida* and *Measure for Measure*. *Richard III* could serve as a practical handbook for the would be tyrant. In a way it already has: the narrative of Hitler's coup runs parallel to the play with uncanny accuracy.

If Shakespeare has what we might call an obsession, it is this: the indissoluble human bond between parents and children – which is simply to say that he was obsessed with the humanness of being human. He believes in the redeeming power of compassion and the transforming, if not always benign, power of love: sexual, fraternal, maternal, paternal; the love of war, of nation, of ambition; all love except love of God. He affirms the infinite ambiguity of people and of nature and takes upon himself the mystery of things as if he were God's spy. Said in other words, what Shakespeare believed is the sum of his plays: to misunderstand that is to misunderstand the role of a playwright. Writers do not have necessarily a set of religious beliefs, but they still have a set of beliefs. The playwright's job is to be able to imagine and describe characters of wildly opposed sensibilities to be able to "invent Rosalind, as fully as Jacques, or Desdemons as fully as Iago." And the actor's job is to inhabit and animate those characters impartially: they must play a character with a child's heart, innocent of judgment. This should be taken for granted, because Shakespeare was a playwright, a producer and above all an actor. So it is precisely this contact with the practicalities of his chosen medium that makes his work so effective. He was not writing for publication. He actually chose to write for the theatre, writing narratives revealed by what people say and do, and engaging the attention of the audience at the instant of performance. He chose to write in verse, although much of many of his plays is in prose. He used verse as an expressive tool that gives a greater pulse, momentum and distillation of thought and feeling, but is no less a medium than prose for delineating character. To appreciate Shakespeare thoroughly is to believe in him as a writer who wrote for the theatre in verse as a matter of choice.

What should be stated with great emphasis is that the life of Shakespeare's plays is in the language, not alongside it or underneath it. Feelings and thoughts are released at the moment of Speech. An Elizabethan audience would have responded to the pulse, the rhythms, the shapes, sounds and meanings, within the consistent ten syllable, five stress lines of blank verse: above all, it was an audience that listened. But that should not surprise us. What is original in Shakespeare is what he did with his material. He was responsible for the invention of distinct, and largely inimitable, forms of plays for which compound words should have been minted. His comedies are comedies in that they are not tragedies: they have happy endings, but most of them are marinated in melancholy, and some of them – *As You Like It* for instance – are not even particularly funny. In the comedies the natural world is strongly evident, not always benign, and streaked with the shadow of tragedy: expulsion from court, shipwreck, war and death. The world is peopled by quite narcissistic young men and strikingly feisty young women, who have a prominence and authority unusual even by the standards of the Twentieth century. The women have frank and realistic attitudes to sex, and are often the cause of sexual competition between male friends. Sex is ever present – a turbulent force that is as much a curse as a blessing: flirtation, courtship, pursuit, cross dressing, gender games, rivalry, jealousy. Invariably, it resolves into the harmony of marriage. Sex in *King Lear* is most of all a great obsession, and it plays the architectonic role in Freud's psychology as power in Hobbes's philosophy. Goneril and Reagan, who are power mad, are sex mad too. They are obsessively secretive and double dealing. The language of power, would it seem, is simple and consists of four letters words. Without these four letters, "you are in Office but not in power!"

Through this reading of *King Lear*, what is to be noted is that Shakespeare's tragedies do not conform totally to any rules of drama, philosophy or religion. Blind fate, the pagan gods, the Christian God, nature itself, all take the blame from time to time for the catastrophe of the lives of the protagonists, but in the end the responsibility of their misfortunes is their own. Consequently, if there is any lesson to be learned from Shakespeare's tragedies it is this: our fate lies in ourselves. *King Lear* is in this case a tragedy about being alive and becoming dead: the smell of mortality. The composer Berlioz, after seeing a performance of *Hamlet* in Paris, said: "Shakespare, coming on me unawares, struck me like a thunderbolt. The lightning flash of that discovery revealed to me at a stroke the whole heaven of art, illuminating it to its remotest corners. I recognised the meaning of grandeur, beauty, dramatic truth... I saw, I understand, I felt... that I was alive and that I must arise and walk... at this time of my life I neither spoke nor understood a word of English." (7)

Exciting new developments in the last few years have changed the face of Shakespeare studies, more suddenly than ever before. Traditional assumptions about Shakespeare's language, ideology, text, have been questioned, often successfully. Greenblatt's *Shakespearean Negotiations* could be one of the examples and great events in literary criticism. Though Greenblatt is an author difficult to deal with, his book is an important and sophisticated interpretation of Shakespeare's plays, reinterpreted according to the "new historicism." A real breakthrough on how to read texts and reinscribe them within a matrix of power and knowledge. What is really new and striking in Greenblatt's approach is the fact that every chapter in the *Negotiations* starts with an anecdote culled from Renaissance scientific works, sermons, and colonialists' tales – a case history, which is analysed brilliantly, revealing implications that less expert readers might well have missed. The anecdote illustrates how Renaissance governments and their agents controlled political or cultural minorities, and Shakespeare's plays of course dramatised similar problems. The anecdote seems to be an essential feature of the "new historicism," anchoring the plays and their problems in something solidly historical. Greenblatt refers to "linkages," and describes the anecdotes as "part of the particular and contingent discourse out of which historically specific subjects were fashioned, represented, and communally incorporated." But what I personally find intriguing and enriching in Greenblatt's interpretation of Shakespeare's plays is the concept of power and the abuse of power. How, for example, the modern state, as represented in the history plays "is shown to be based upon acts of calculation, intimidation, and deceit;" how the "betrayal of friends does not subvert but rather sustains the moral authority and the compelling glamour of power;" how the theatre thrives on disrespect, even disrespect to itself, with all those clowns, and subplots that parody the main plot, etc. And whether or not we agree with every part of Greenblatt's *Negotiations*, this book remains an impressive achievement. Despite some jumps in the argument here and there, Greenblatt offers many new insights into Elizabethan social pressures, with his many suggestive explanations.

If Bloom, in *The Western Canon* aired the notion that Shakespeare "invented us," his thesis – in *Shakespeare: The Invention of the Human* – is that Shakespeare, who is much greater than any other writer and much more intelligent than any thinker in any discipline, invented what we define as personality by inventing characters of unlimited depth, interiority, and self creation. According to him, only Chaucer comes close to doing this before Shakespeare, and Shakespeare's contemporaries show nothing of his confounding of art and nature. Freud, in such a view, just plagiarises Shakespeare, as we do all. At the same time, Bloom presents one of the boldest theses of Shakespearean scholarships, that Shakespeare not only invented the English language, but also created human nature as we know it today. So before Shakespeare there was characterisation; after Shakespeare, there were characters, men and women capable of change, with highly individual personalities.

Scholars have been combing through Shakespeare's works for centuries. The growth in Shakespeare criticism is exponential. Thousands of articles, monographs, and books on Shakespeare are published every year. Critics of all schools are still searching for an answer to the question "Who is Shakespeare?" Is he primarily a man of the theatre, as he is in Bernard Beckerman's "Shakespeare at the Globe"? Is he a closet Catholic, as Eric Sams believes? Was he gay, as a number of critics of the *Sonnets* hold? Is he a writer obsessed with his position at court, as Alvin Kernan writes? While it is certain that every age will produce its own interpretations, its own Shakespeare(s), it grows less and less likely that someone will come up with some sort of archeological find, a riddle answered. Scholars are still poking around the question of authorship, the possibility that someone else – Bacon; or De Vere, the Earl of Oxford; or someone quite obscure – wrote one or more of the plays now attributed to Shakespeare. Once in a great while, a scholar believes he has added to the existing Shakespeare canon by discovering a lost manuscript attributable to the Master. In 1985, Gary Taylor, a professor at Brandeis University, did that when he found a poem in Oxford's Bodleian Library called "Shall I Die? Shall I fly?" Taylor was convinced that the poem, though not an especially good one, was Shakespeare's. His discovery sparked much dissent and at least as much jealousy in the academic world – especially after it was publicised on the front page of the *Times*. A few years later, after the furor had subsided, he wrote an article for the *Times* recalling the strange interplay between scholarship and its interpretation in the press: "Literary scholarship, like journalism, is a competitive business. New theories do not, and should not, win instant unanimous acceptance. So whenever a new theory is pronounced, in literature or in science, rival experts will leap to attack it. Every newborn theory has to fight for its life. That war of theories goes on all the time, whether or not journalists become involved. The press simply accelerates, exaggerates and personalises the struggle." (8)

Shakespeare's duplicitous manipulations of words – in his tragic plays in general and his *Sonnets* in particular –, as they are made either to move outward to interanimate one another or to move inward to cut off from themselves – or to manage somehow to do both at once — arise from his struggle to win from language a representational power that he does not trust words normally to provide. By exploiting mainly the sensory side of words – their sound, which is their only material aspect – Shakespeare the poet tries to invoke the illusion of their presence: he uses the sensible to transform the intelligible. It is his way to overcome our impression of verbal absence – inspired by an exclusive interest in the merely intelligible aspect of words – our impressions of words whose object is elsewhere as they mean, often vainly, to point to it. Thus their auditory character, normally most arbitrary in that it has no relation to their meaning, seems to turn words substantive, in effect allows them to take on the illusion of body. So apparently, acknowledging normal language to be a verbal parade of arbitrary meanings, of empty, bodiless counters, Shakespeare seeks to turn the arbitrary into the necessary and the functional into the materially present. Shall we point Philip Sidney's Sonnet 35 "What may words say, or what may words not say?" Maybe this could be a clue to see better the problem of representation and the futile contribution made by our usual words to solving it. Shakespeare has always and already discovered the built in futility of our usual attempt at verbal representation. That futility is

carried in the prefix, the *re* of *re*present. Words are empty and belated counters because it is their nature to seek to refer to what is elsewhere and has occurred earlier. Any pretension by them to present reality is frustrated by the *re*, which requires that what they would represent – what has already presented itself in person – has had its presence, its presentness, elsewhere and earlier [...] But the poet would dabble in verbal magic, calling upon a sacred name that would overcome belatedness and introduce a living, bodily hereness that would make language more than properly representational; that would make it nothing less than presentational. (Krieger 214)

What is it that makes Shakespeare different? Is it his poetry? Or his characters? Or his invisibility, emptying the plays so entirely of his own views and opinions that they are infinitely reinterpretable? Frank Kermode in his last book on Shakespeare, (9) tries to answer these questions with masterly directness. He argues that something extraordinary happened to Shakespeare in mid-career. Shakespeare abandoned that formal rhetoric imprint of the early plays, and seemed to embrace a new way of representing emotionally agitated thought that was unlike anything in previous world literature. This new language of Shakespeare, these violent images, bypass coherent explanation or decipherment. There looms a new language which reflects the confused possibilities and insoluble dilemmas that underlie rational thought – a real portrayal of thought happening. This new Shakespearean language – adds Kermode – is an obsessive, self indulgent passion for the repetition and interchiming of particular words. In Hamlet, this takes the form of a persistent rhetorical device that splits a single thought into words or phrases, and all the play's passionate and moody broodings revert to this one into two pattern. It is as if Shakespeare's fascination with a particular word-pattern came first, and determined the kind of people he should invent and the deeds he should make them form. Yet with Shakespeare, Kermode argues, the obsession could become inhuman, like the fascination of a great mathematician with numbers. *King Lear* particularly shocks him, by allowing a language pattern to irrupt into dramatic action, as the text's relentless emphasis on eyes and seeing culminates in the blinding of Gloucester. For Kermode – and it is hard to disagree – there is something sadistic about an author who could pursue his word games to such a conclusion. (10) Kermode – as Allen Lane reports – is especially interested in what he calls the new style that began to show itself in *Richard II* and *Henry IV* and bloomed into the kinetic, knotted, dangerous soliloquies of *Macbeth*, *Hamlet* and *King Lear*. This new style, characterised by an intense brooding on sets of words and images, at times "takes the poet beyond the limits of reason and intelligibility."

Language does but violate its obligation to have a unity of meaning: the criteria of what is true are shrewdly double. The old notion of truth that we used to call "troth" (or faith) resists the newer truths unmodified by faith in a historical conflict between world views and concepts of value. Should we not value, and set aside for separate and fragmented treatment, those specially constructed objects that seem addressed to the aesthetic need? How can we have any but an ambiguous ontological sense of what is unfolding before us? What is the reality of a Lear who suffers and dies every night and yet is still there because his death is not as ours is to be, even though we must also think of his death as absolute (like ours) if we are to take the dramatic illusion seriously, as we do? Do we suffer for him because we know our reality must not intrude upon his? Do we affirm presence only as an illusion, which is to admit that it is not – in another sense – present at all? Perhaps drama – as Murray seems to maintain – with its peculiar conjunctions of reality and make believe, works to remind us of the unstable relation between presence and illusion in all signifier/signified relations. Hence, with this process of affirming and denying, we move into the infinite regress of illusions within illusions, or presence within presences – as the distinction between presence and illusion blurs before us. In this endless struggle, aesthetic presentation brings only what seems to function as no more than self effacing materials of representation.

NOTES

PART ONE

(1) Jacques Derrida, "Aphorism Countertime" in *Acts of Literature*, New York: Routledge, 1992, p. 133. It should be emphasised here that as proved in particular by the later renewal of antisystematic thought in Hamman, the Romantics, Nietzsche, and many others, the aesthetic of the fragment pre-supposes the early determination of philosophy as episteme, and hence the systematic exposition and construction of systems. As a matter of fact, this antisystematic, fragmentary practice is in no sense radically subversive of the idea of science or of systematicity as characteristic of the philosophical enterprise; it is, rather, a genuine possibility within philosophy itself, and it carries out the systematic requirements of philosophy in its own way.

(2) J.J. Mayoux, *Shakespeare*, Paris: Aubier Montaigne, 1983, p. 122. John Keats, a name that releases a flood of familiar images, apostle of beauty and truth of negative capability whose march of passion and en-deavour is a combination of suffering and striving, has always believed that there are good reasons that Love always fuses into Death. It is this capacity, or more precisely this ability to negate or lose one's identity in something larger than oneself which Shakespeare possessed so enormously and which Keats felt was lacking in much of the poetry of his own day. The object of poetry for Keats is the identity, the nature or truth of individual, or what Gerard Manley Hopkins later called Inscape.

(3) "The Writer is someone who plays with the mother's body [...]: in order to glorify it, to embellish it, or in order to dismember it, to take it to the limit of what can be known about the body: I would go so far as to take bliss in a disfiguration of the language." Roland Barthes, *The Pleasure of the Text*, trans. Richard Miller, New York: Hill and Wang, 1975, p. 37. For an excellent overview of contemporary theories of play and the early psychological development of the self, see Anna Nardo, *The Ludic Self in Seventeenth-Century English Literature*, Albany: SUNY Press, 1991. Anna Nardo offers pertinent speculations about the cultural contexts of the idea

of "play" in the early modern period. Another reference, an earlier source is Anna Righter's *Shakespeare and the Idea of the Play*, London: Chatto and Windus, 1964; see in particular the sections on "Play or Illusion" and "The Play Metaphor" (pp. 57 – 63; 64 – 86). Another reference to the ideas and practices of play in society and language, see James Hans, *The Play of the World*, Amherst: University of Massachusetts Press, 1981. Hans plays the deconstructionist here, but he also maintains agency and intention as essential human attributes that orient and direct language even as they are directed by it. According to his thesis, like "free association," the free play of language is not absolutely free. It is bounded on one side by personal desire and on another by social communication. "Play" appears therefore as a serious gaming for it points to the fundamental activity of man, a movement of encounter and exchange with the world, out of which understanding comes.

(4) See Jacques Derrida, "La Main de Heidegger" in *Heidegger et la question*, Paris: Flammarion, 1990.

(5) See René Descartes, *Discourse on Method and the Meditations*, trans. F. E. Sutcliffe, Harmondsworth: Penguin, 1968, Discourse 4.

(6) See Merleau-Ponty, *The Visible and the Invisible*, trans. Alphonso Lingis, Evanson: Northwestern University Press, 1968.

(7) B. McElroy, *Shakespeare's Mature Tragedies*, New Jersey: Princeton University Press, 1973, p. 175. It should be noted here and without delving into more details that the fragmentation vision in *King Lear*, and especially in Lear's mind replaces a single totalising vision of the world with a plurality of such world views, each complete and all embracing, and precisely for this reason closed to and incommensurable with one another. What Lear envisons is essentially the idea that it is possible to have a complete, all embracing world view. Lear strives to impose order on the world, struggling to domesticate and shape it. Only fragments, pieces remain in Lear's grasp. Everything seems to resist and exceed his hold. In seeking to order the world, Lear inevitably comes up against that which is other. But such a behaviour does not exclude the other; on the contrary, it calls for dialogue. It involves a reciprocity, a two-way, back and forth movement or interplay between Lear himself and the world. What is at issue here is the liberating, problematising, and unpredictable potential of conversation, which is capable of leading us to new insights and critical self reflection

through experiencing the Other, or an Other: Lear. If Lear seems to come up against that which is Other, such a behaviour enables us to explore the complex nexus that underlies every act of understanding in the unity of interpretive consciousness, pre-understanding, and language.

PART TWO

(1) M. Heidegger, "Nihilism, Nihil and Nothing" in *Nietzsche*, trans. David Farrell, San Francisco: Harper San Francisco, 1991, vol. 4, p. 18. Shakespeare's use of "nothing" in *King Lear* and also in *Hamlet* has been pointed out by many commentators. See among many others, Eric Partridge, Shakespeare's Bawdy, rev. ed. (London: Routledge and Kegan Paul, 1968). It has been assumed by most critics that the word "thing" in itself is meaningless, and it can fill in any blank, replacing any other noun. David Willbern, for example, reminds us that in Judaeo Christian mythology, the Beginning is characterised by a void (Old Testament), and by a word (New Testament). The two myths together create the primary dialect of void and word, nothing and noting, which Joyce captures in his most significant pun in *Finnegans Wake*: "In the beginning is the woid, in the muddle is the sounddance." Jacques Derrida's philosophy relates eloquently these "primordial absence and zero degree writing." At a certain point, Derrida calls these representatives phantoms or ghosts. "Nothings," phantoms or ghosts are the shapes of that from which logic proceeds. They seem, as a matter of fact, to betray their subjection to the logic that they underground. These ghosts represent the excluded Other from the system, and are its negative key, its Other. (See J. Derrida, *Dissemination*, trans. B. Johnson, Chicago: University of Chicago Press, 1981, pp. 103–104).

(2) Patricia Ondek Laurence, *The Reading of Silence*: *Virginia Woolf in the English Tradition*, Stanford, California: Stanford University Press, 1991, p. 6. It seems that silence is the very ground of any literary production. Writes Pierre Macherey: "The speech of a book comes from a certain silence, a matter which it endows with form, a ground on which it traces a figure. Thus, the book is not self sufficient; it is necessarily accompanied by a certain absence, without which it would not exist. A knowledge of the book must include a consideration of this absence. This is why it seems useful and legitimate to ask of every production what it tacitly implies, what it does not say."

(*A Theory of Literary Production*, trans. Geoffrey Wall, London: Routledge and Kegan Paul, 1978, p. 85).

(3) E. Ionesco, "Journal", in G. Steiner, *Language and Silence*, London: Pelican Books, 1969, p. 74.

(4) Lacan, *Ecrits* pp. 90–91. It must be noted here that the mirror functions as an instrument of disclosure (dévoilement). It discloses itself because of the orientation of the subject's eyes; at the same time, the mirror discloses and conceals, it makes visible and invisible.

(5) Writes Montaigne: "Mais il n'y a rien d'inutile dans la nature, pas même l'inutilité elle-même; rien ne s'est inséré dans cet univers qui n'y tienne une place opportune. L'être que nous sommes est cimenté de façons d'être maladives; l'ambition, la jalousie, l'envie, la vengeance, la superstition, le désespoir logent en nous avec une possession si naturelle que l'image de cela se reconnaît aussi chez les bêtes; il y a même la cruauté, vice si dénaturé: car, au milieu de la compassion, nous entendons au dedans de nous je ne sais quelle pointe de plaisir méchant à voir souffrir autrui. [...] Les philosophes, avec raison nous renvoient aux règles de la Nature; mais celles-ci n'ont que faire d'une aussi sublime connaissance; ils les falsifient et ils nous présentent le visage de la Nature peint trop haut en couleur et trop sophistiqué: de là naissent un très grand nombre de portraits différents d'un sujet aussi uniforme. [...] Se confier le plus simplement à la Nature, c'est s'y confier le plus sagement. Oh! que c'est un doux et mol oreiller, et sain, que l'ignorance et l'insouciance d'apprendre pour reposer une tête bien faite." Montaigne, *Essais, Livre III*, Translation in Modern French by André Lanly, Paris: Editions Champion, 1989, pp. 7–281.

(6) Writes Sidney: "There is no art delivered to mankind that hath not the works of Nature for his principal project, without which they could not consist, and on which they so depend, as they become actors and players, as it were, of what Nature will have set forth. So doth the musician in time tell you which by nature agree, which not. The natural philosopher thereon hath his name, and the moral philosopher standeth upon the natural virtues, vices, and passions of man; and 'follow Nature' (saith he) 'therein, and thou soul shalt not err.' [...] And the metaphysic, though it be in the second and abstract notions, and therefore be counted supernatural, yet doth he indeed build upon the depth of Nature. [...] Neither let it be deemed too saucy a comparison to balance the highest point of man's wit with the efficacy of

Nature; but rather give right honour to the heavenly Maker of that maker, who, having made man to His own likeness, set him beyond and over all works of that second nature: which in nothing he showeth so much as in Poetry, when with the force of a divine breath he bringeth forth far surpassing her doings, with no small argument to the incredulous of that first accursed fall of Adam, since our erected wit maketh us know what perfection is, and yet our infected will keepeth us from reaching unto it." Sir Philip Sydney, "An Apology of Poetry," in *Criticism: The Major Texts*, ed. Walter Jackson Bate & Abbott Lawrence Lowell, New York: Harcourt, Brace & World, INC, 1952, pp. 85–86.

(7) "The Avon Catalogue" in *The Guardian Saturday Review*, September 4, 1999, p.18.

(8) Gary Taylor, quoted in *The New Yorker*, November 20, 1995, p. 80.

(9) Frank Kermode, *Shakespeare's Language*, London: Penguin, 2000. Writes Kermode: "It is curious that this play, which it is surely impossible for anybody who cares about poetry to write on without some expression of awe, should offer few of the local excitements to be found, say, in the narrower context of *Measure for Measure*. The explanation must be that the subjects of *King Lear* reflect a much more general, indeed a universal tragedy. In *King Lear* we are no longer concerned with an ethical problem that, however agonising, can be reduced to an issue of law or equity and discussed forensically. For *King Lear* is about suffering represented as a condition of the world as we inherit it or make it for ourselves." (p. 184)

(10) See John Carey "A Way with Words," *The Sunday Times Culture*, May 21, 2000, p. 36–37.

BIBLIOGRAPHY

Adelman, Janet, *Suffocating Fantasies of Maternal Origin in Shakespeare's Plays, Hamlet to The Tempest*, New York: Routledge, 1992.

Adorno, Theodor, *Negative Dialectics*, trans. E.B. Ashton, New York: Seabury Press, 1973.

Aers, David, *Community, Gender, and Individual Identity: English Writing 1360–1430*, London: Routledge, 1988.

Alexander, Nigel, *Poison, Play and Duel*, London: Routledge/Kegan Paul, 1971.

Ariès, Philippe, *Western Attitudes toward Death*, trans. Patricia Ranum, Baltimore: Johns Hopkins University Press, 1974.

Atkins, G. Douglas, and Bergeron, David M. (eds.), *Shakespeare and Deconstruction*, New York: Peter Lang, 1988.

Austin, J.L., *How to Do Things with Words,* Oxford: Oxford University Press, 1962.

Aydelotte, Frank, *Elisabethan Rogues and Vagabonds*, New York: Barnes and Noble, 1967.

Barkan, Leonard, *Nature's Work of Art: The Human Body as Image of the World*, New Haven, Conn.: Yale University Press, 1975.

Barker, Francis, *The Tremulous Private Body: Essays on Subjection*, London/New York: Methuen, 1984.

Barker, Philip, *Michel Foucault: Subversions of the Subject*, St Leonards: Allen and Unwin, 1994.

Barker, Stephen, *Auto-Aesthetics: Strategies of the Self After Nietzsche*, New Jersey/London: Humanities Press, 1992.

Barthes, Roland, *Critique et vérité*, Paris: Seuil, 1966.

—, *The Pleasure of the Text*, trans. Richard Miller, New York: Hill & Wang, 1975.

—, *The Rustle of Language*, trans. Richard Howard, Berkeley/Los Angeles: University of California Press, 1989.

Bataille, Georges, *Vision of Excess: Selected Writings 1927–39,* Minneapolis: University of Minnesota Press, 1985.

Bateson, Gregory, *Mind and Nature: A Necessary Unity,* New York: Dutton, 1979.

Baudrillard, Jean, *Simulations,* New York: Semiotext, 1983.

Beier, A.L., *Masterless Men: The Vagrancy Problem in England 1560–1640*, London: Methuen, 1985.

Belsey, Catherine, *The Subject of Tragedy*, London: Routledge, 1985.

Benhabib, Seyla, "The Generalised and Concrete Other", in Eva Feder Kittay and Diana T. Meyers (eds.), *Women and Moral Theory*, New Jersey: Rowman and Littlefield, 1987.

—, *Situating the Self: Gender, Community and Postmodernism in Contemporary Ethics*, Cambridge: Polity, 1992.

Bennet, Susan, *Performing Nostalgia: Shifting Shakespeare and the Contemporary Past*, London: Routledge, 1996.

Berger, Harry, *Imaginary Audition: Shakespeare on Stage and Page*, Berkeley: University of California Press, 1989.

Bernauer, James, "Foucault's Ecstatic Thinking", in James Bauer and David Ramussen (eds.), *The Final Foucault*, Cambridge, MA: MIT Press, 1988.

Bevington, David, *Action Is Eloquence: Shakespeare's Language of Gesture*, Cambridge, MA: Harvard University Press, 1984.

Bhabha, Homi K., *The Location of Culture*, London/New York: Routledge, 1994.

Bident, Christophe, *Maurice Blanchot: Partenaire invisible*, Paris: Champ Vallon, 1998.

Blau, Herbert, *Take Up the Bodies: Theater at the Vanishing Point*, Urbana: University of Illinois Press, 1982.

Blanchot, Maurice, *Comment la littérature est-elle possible?,* Paris: Corti, 1942.

—, *Faux pas*, Paris: Gallimard, 1943.

—, *La part du,* Paris: Gallimard, 1949.

—, *La Folie du jour*, Montpellier: Fata Morgana, 1973.

—, *L'Ecriture du désastre*, Paris: Gallimard, 1980.

—, *Le Pas au-delà*, Paris: Gallimard, 1973.

—, *Michel Foucault tel que je l'imagine*, Montpellier, 1986.

Blayney, Peter W.M., *The Texts of King Lear and their Origins*, Cambridge: Cambridge University Press, 1982.

Bloom, Harold, *The Western Canon: The Books and School of the Ages*, New Yok: Harcourt Brace, 1994.

—, *L'amour et l'amitié,* Paris: Editions de Fallois, 1996.

Bogue, Ronald, *Deleuze and Guattari*, London: Routledge, 1989.

Boothby, Richard, *Death and Desire*, New York: Routledge, 1991.

Borch-Jacobsen, Mikkel, *Lacan le maître absolu,* Paris: Flammarion, 1995.

Bowie, Malcolm, *Freud, Proust and Lacan: Theory as Fiction*, Cambridge, New York: Cambridge University Press, 1987.

Bracher, Mark, ed alt. (eds.), *Lacanian Theory of Discourse*, New York and London: New York University Press, 1994.

Bradley, Andrew Cecil, *Shakespearean Tragedy*, New York: Fawcett Premier, 1965.

Bristol, Michael D., *Shakespeare's America: America's Shakespeare*, London: Routledge, 1990.

Brooks, Peter, *Body Work. Objects of Desire in Modern Narrative*, Cambridge, MA, London: Harvard University Press, 1993.

Brown, Peter, *The Body and Society: Men, Women, and Sexual Renunciation in Early Christianity*, New York: Columbia University Press, 1988.

Bulman, James C. (ed.), *Shakespeare, Theory, and Performance*, London: Routledge, 1996.

Burgess, Anthony, *Re Joyce*, New York: Norton, 1965.

Callaghan, Dympna, *Women and Gender in Renaissance Tragedy: A Study of King Lear, Othello, The Duchess of Malfi and the White Devil*, New York: Harvester Wheatsheaf, 1989.

Caroll, John, *Humanism: The Wreck of Western Culture*, London: Fontana, 1993.

Carruthers, Mary, *The Book of Memory: A Study of Memory in Medieval Culture*, Cambridge: Cambridge University Press, 1990.

Cartwright, Kent, *Shakespearean Tragedy and its Double: The Rhythms of Audience Response*, Pennsylvania: Pennsylvania State University Press, 1991.

Cavell, Stanley, *Disowing Knowledge in Six Plays of Shakespeare*, Cambridge: Cambridge University Press, 1987.

Chambers, Edmund Kercherver, *William Shakespeare: A Study of Facts and Problems*, Oxford: Clarendon Press, 1990.

Charnes, Linda, *Notorious Identity: Materializing the Subject in Shakespeare*, Cambridge, MA: Harvard University Press, 1993.

Chebel, Malek, *La Féminisation du monde: Essai sur les mille et une nuits*, Paris, Payot, 1996.

Cixous, Hélène, *Le Troisième corps*, Paris: Grasset, 1970.

—, *Stigmata. Escaping Texts*, London/New York: Routledge, 1998.

Clemen, Wolfgang, *The Development of Shakespeare's Imagery*, London: Methuen and CO LTD, 1977.

Coles, Romand, *Self/Power/Other: Political Theory and Dialogical Ethics*, Ithaca: Cornell University Press, 1992.

Colie, Rosalie, and Flahiff, F.T. (eds.), *Some Facets of King Lear: Essays in Prismatic Criticism,* Toronto and London: University of Toronto Press, 1974.

Coupland, Douglas, *Microserfs,* London: Flamingo, 1996.

Cressy, David, *Literacy and Social Order: Reading and Writing in Tudor and Stuart England*, Cambridge: Cambridge University Press, 1980.

D'Amico, Robert, *Historicism and Knowledge,* New York, London: Routledge, 1989.

Daley, Mary, *Outercourse: The Be-Dazzling Voyage*, New York: Harper Collins, 1992.

Dauphiné, James, *Les structures symboliques dans le théâtre de Shakespeare*, Paris: Les Belles Lettres, 1983.

Davidson, Donald, *Inquiries into Truth and Interpretation*, Oxford: Clarendon Press, 1984.

Delannoi, Gil, "Shakespeare et le naturel", in *Esprit* n. 235, Août-Septembre, 1997.

Deleuze, Gilles, Guattari, Félix, *Mille Plateux: capitalisme et schizophrénie*, Paris: Minuit, 1980.

Deleuze, Gilles, *Logique du sens*, Paris: Minuit, 1969.

—, *Critique et clinique*, Paris: Minuit, 1993.

—, *Nietzsche and Philosophy*, trans. Hugh Tomlinson, London: Athlone, 1983.

De Man, Paul, *Allegories of Reading*, New Haven and London: Yale University Press, 1979.

—, *Blindness and Insight. Essays in the Rhetoric of Contemporary Criticism*, Minneapolis: University of Minnesota Press, 1983.

Derrida, Jacques, *Acts of Literature*, New York: Routledge, 1992.

—, *Dissemination*, trans. B. Johnson, Chicago: University of Chicago Press, 1981.

—, *Glas*, Paris: Denoël/Gonthier, 1981.

—, *Glas*, trans. Leavey and Rand, Lincoln: University of Nebraska Press, 1982.

—, *Heidegger et la question*, Paris: Flammarion, 1990.

—, *La voix et le phénomène*, Paris: Quadrigue/PUF, 1993.

—, *Le monolinguisme de l'autre*, Paris: Galilée, 1996.

—, *Mal d'Archive. Une impression freudienne*, Paris: Galilée, 1995.

—, *Margins of Philosophy*, New York: F. Ungar, 1967.

—, *Of Grammatology*, Baltimore & London: The Johns Hopkins University Press, 1967.

—, *On the Name*, trans. David Wood, John P. Leavey, Jr., and Ian McLeod, Stanford, CA: Stanford University Press, 1995.

—, *Otobiographies*, Paris: Galilée, 1984.

—, *Points de suspension. Entretiens*, Paris: Galilée, 1992.

—, *Psyché. Inventions de l'autre*, Paris: Galilée, 1987.

—, *Spurs: Nietzsche's Styles*, trans. B. Harlow, Chicago: University of Chicago Press, 1979.

—, *The Ear of the Other*, trans. Avital Ronell (ed), Christie McDonald, New York: Schocken, 1985.

—, "How to avoid Speaking?" in *Languages of the Unsayable: The Play of Negativity in Literature and Literary Theory*, Sanford Budick & Wolfgang Iser (eds.), New York: Columbia University Press, 1989.

Descartes, René, *Discourse on Method and the Meditations*, trans. F.E. Sutcliffe, Harmondsworth: Penguin, 1968.

Desmet, Christy, *Reading Shakespeare's Characters: Rhetoric, Ethics, and Identity*, Amherst: University of Massachusetts Press, 1992.

Diprose, Rosalyn, and Ferrell, Robyn (eds.), *Cartographies: Posmodernism and the Mapping of Bodies and Spaces*, Sydney: Allen and Unwin, 1991.

Dollimore, Jonathan, and Sinfield, Alan (eds.), *Political Shakespeare: New*

Essays in Cultural Materialism, Manchester: Manchester University Press, 1985.

—, *Radical Tragedy: Religion, Ideology and Power in the Drama of Shakespeare and his Contemporaries,* Brighton: Harvest, 1984.

—, *Death, Desire and Loss in Western Culture,* London: Penguin, 1998.

Drakakis, John (ed.), *Alternative Shakespeares,* London: Routledge, 1985.

Eagleton, Terry, *William Shakespeare,* Oxford: Blackwell, 1986.

Eco, Umberto, *I limiti dell'interpretazione,* Milano: Bompiani, 1990.

Eisaman Maus, Katherine, *Inwardness and Theater in the English Renaissance,* Chicago: University of Chicago Press, 1995.

Eliot, T.S., *Elizabethan Dramatists,* London: Faber and Faber LTD, 1962.

Enterline, Lynn, *The Rhetoric of the Body From Ovid To Shakespeare,* Cambridge: Cambridge University Press, 2000.

Erickson, Peter, *Patriarchal Studies in Shakespeare's Drama,* Berkeley, CA, London: University of California Press, 1985.

Evans, G. Blackmore, (ed.), *Shakespeare: Aspects of Influence,* Cambridge, MA: Harvard University Press, 1976.

Evans, Malcolm, *Signifying Nothing,* Brighton: Harvester, 1988.

Falzon, Christopher, *Foucault and Social Dialogue,* London and New York: Routledge, 1998.

Farrell, Kirby, *Shakespeare's Creation: The Language of Magic and Play,* Amherst: University of Massachusetts Press, 1975.

Felman, Shoshana, *Writing and Madness,* trans. Martha Noel Evans, Ithaca: Cornell University Press, 1985.

Fineman, Joel, *Shakespeare's Perjured Eye: The Invention of Poetic Subjectivity in the Sonnets,* Berkeley: University of California Press, 1986.

Flax, Jane, *Thinking Fragments: Psychoanalysis, Feminism and Postmodernism in the Contemporary West,* Berkeley: University of California Press, 1990.

Foakes, R.A., *Hamlet Versus Lear. Cultural Politics and Shakespeare's Art,* Cambridge: Cambridge University Press, 1993.

Foucault, Michel, *Discipline and Punish: The Birth of a Prison,* trans. Alan Sherida, New York: Pantheon, 1977.

—, *Feminism and Foucault,* Irene Diamond and Lee Quinby (eds.), Boston: Northeastern University Press, 1988.

—, *Language, Countermemory, Practice, Selected Essays and Interviews*, Ithaca, New York: Cornell University Press, 1977.

Freedman, Barbara, *Staging the Gaze: Postmodernism, Psychoanalysis and Shakespearean Comedy*, Ithaca, New York: Cornell University Press, 1991.

French, Marilyn, *Shakespeare's Division of Experience*, London: Cape, 1982.

Frese, Dolores Warwick and O'Keefe, Katherine O'Brien, *The Book and The Body*, Indiana/London: University of Notre Dame Press, 1997.

Frye, Northrop, *Fools of Time*, Toronto: University of Toronto Press, 1981.

Gadamer, Hans-Georg, *Truth and Method,* trans. Joe Weinsheimer & Donald G. Maeshall, New York: Crossroad, 1991.

Gallop, Jane, *Thinking Through the Body*, New York: Columbia University Press, 1988.

Garber, Marjorie, *Shakespeare's Ghost Writers: Literature as Uncanny Causality,* New York: Methuen, 1987.

Gasché, Rodolphe, *Inventions of Difference On Jacques Derrida*, Cambridge, MA, London: Harvard University Press, 1994.

—, *The Tain of the Mirror. Derrida and the Philosophy of Reflection*, Cambridge, MA, London: Harvard University Press, 1986.

Genette, Gérard, *Palimpsestes: La littérature au second degré*, Paris: Seuil, 1982.

Germain, Sylvie, *Les échos du silence*, Paris: Desclée de Brouwer, 1996.

Gillies, John, *Shakespeare and the Geography of Difference*, Cambridge: Cambridge University Press, 1994.

Girard, René, *Shakespeare: les feux de l'envie*, Paris: Bernard Grasset, 1990.

Goldberg, S.L., *An Essay on King Lear*, Cambridge, London, New York: Cambridge University Press, 1980.

Golomb, Jacob, *Nietzsche's Enticing Psychology of Power*, Ames: Iowa State University Press, 1987.

Grady, Hugh (ed.), *Shakespeare and Modernity. Early Modern to Millennium*, London/New York: Routledge, 2000.

Grady, Hugh, *The Modernist Shakespeare*, Oxford: Oxford University Press, 1991.

Green, André, *Hamlet et* Hamlet: *Une interprétation psychanalytique de la représentation*, Paris: Balland, 1982.

Greenblatt, Stephen, *Learning to Curse: Essays in Early Modern Culture*, London: Routledge, 1991.

—, *Renaissance Self-Fashioning,* Chicago: Chicago University Press, 1980.

—, *Shakespearean Negotiations: The Circulation of Social Energy in Renaissance England*, Oxford: Clarendon Press, 1988.

—(ed.), *Representing the English Renaissance*, Berkeley: University of California Press, 1988.

Hacking, Ian, *Why Does Language Matter to Philosophy?,* Cambridge: Cambridge University Press, 1975.

Haegel, Pascal, *Le Corps quel défi pour la personne*, Paris: Fayard, 1999.

Halio, Jay L. (ed.), *The Tragedy of King Lear*, Cambridge: Cambridge University Press, 1992.

Hans, James, *The Play of the World*, Amherst: University of Massachusetts Press, 1981.

Hapgood, Robert, *Shakespeare the Theatre-Poet*, Oxford: Clarendon, 1988.

Hardison, Jr, O.B., (ed.), *The Quest for Imagination: Essays in Twentieth-Century Aesthetic Criticism*, Cleveland: Case Western Reserve University Press, 1971.

Hartman, Geoffrey H., *Criticism in the Wilderness. The Study of Literature Today*, New Haven and London: Yale University Press, 1980.

—, *The Fate of Reading*, Chicago: University of Chicago Press, 1975.

Hawkes, Terence, *Meaning by Shakespeare*, London: Routledge, 1992.

—, *Shakespeare's Talking Animals: Language and Drama in Society,* London: Edward Arnold, 1973.

—, *That Shakespearean Rag,* London: Routledge, 1986.

—, *William Shakespeare King Lear*, London: Northcote House Publishers, 1995.

Heidegger, Martin, *Being and Time*, Oxford: Blackwell, 1962.

—, *Nietzsche*, trans. David Farrell, San Francisco: Harper San Francisco, 1991.

—, *The Question of Being,* trans. W. Kluback and J.T. Wilde, New York: Twayne, 1958.

—, *What Is Called Thinking*, trans. J. Glenn Gray, New York: Harper & Row Publishers, 1971.

Hodgdon, Barbara, *The End Crowns All: Closure and Contradictions in Shakespeare's History*, Princeton: Princeton University Press, 1991.

Howard, Jean E., and O'Connor, Marion F. (eds.), *Shakespeare Reproduced: The Text in History and Ideology*, London: Routledge, 1988.

—, *The Stage and Social Struggle in Early Modern England,* London: Routledge, 1994.

Hoy, David Couzens, *The Critical Circle*, Berkeley, Los Angeles, London: University of California Press, 1978.

Hume, David, *Treatise of Human Nature*, edited by L.A. Selby-Bigge, Oxford: Clarendon Press, 1978.

Hunter, G.K., *Dramatic Identities and Cultural Tradition: Studies on Shakespeare and His Contemporaries*, New York: Harper, 1978.

Hussey, S.S., *The Literary Language of Shakespeare*, Essex: Longman, 1982.

Huston, Hollis, *The Actor's Instrument: Body, Theory, Stage*, Ann Arbor: University of Michigan Press, 1992.

Ibn Arabi, Mohyieddin, *L'interprète des désirs*, trans. Maurice Gloton, Paris: Albin Michel, 1996.

Irigaray, Lucy, *Le Corps-à-corps avec la mère*, Montreal: Les Editions de la Pleine Lune, 1981.

—, *Marine Lover of Friedrich Nietzsche*, trans. G.C. Gill, New York: Cambridge University Press, 1991.

Jardine, Lisa, *Reading Shakespeare Historically*, London: Routledge, 1996.

Johnson, Barbara, "Rigorous Unreliability," in *Critical Inquiry 2*, 1984.

Johnson, Christopher, *System and Writing in the Philosophy. Jacques Derrida*, Cambridge: Cambridge University Press, 1993.

Johnson, David, *Shakespeare and South Africa*, Oxford: Clarendon, 1996.

Jouve, Vincent, *La littérature selon Barthes*, Paris: Minuit, 1986.

Kahn, Coppelia, "The Absent Mother in *King Lear*", in Margaret Ferguson, Maureen Quilligan, and Nancy Vikers (eds.), *Rewriting the Renaissance: The Discourse of Sexual Difference in Early Europe*, Chicago: University of Chicago Press, 1986.

—, *Man's Estate: Masculine Identity in Shakespeare,* Berkeley, CA.: California University Press, 1981.

Kermode, Frank, *Forms of Attention*, Chicago: Chicago University Press, 1985.

—, *Shakespeare's Language*, London: Penguin, 2000.

Klemm, E. David, *The Hermeneutical Theory of Paul Ricoeur*, London & Toronto: Bucknell University Press, 1983.

Koelb, Clayton and Noakes, Susan (eds.), *The Comparative Perspective on Literature*, Ithaca and London: Cornell University Press, 1988.

Kott, Jan, *Shakespeare Our Contemporary*, London: Methuen & CO LTD, 1967.

Krieger, Murray, *Poetic Presence and Illusion: Essays in Critical History and Theory*, Baltimore: The Johns Hopkins University Press, 1979.

—, *Words about Words about Words: Theory, Criticism and the Literary Text*, Baltimore/London: The Johns Hopkins University Press, 1988.

Kristeva, Julia, *Black Sun: Depression and Melancholia*, trans. Leon Roudiez, New York: Columbia University Press, 1989.

—, *Le langage, cet inconnu*, Paris: Seuil, 1981.

—, *Soleil noir*, Paris: Gallimard, 1987.

Krupnik, Mark (ed.), *Displacement: Derrida and After*, Bloomington: Indiana University Press, 1983.

Lacan, Jacques, *Ecrits*, Paris: Seuil, 1966.

—, *The Language of the Self: The Function of Language in Psychoanalysis*, trans. with notes and commentary by Anthony Wilden, Baltimore: Johns Hopkins University Press, 1968.

Laqueur, Thomas, *Making Sex: Body and Gender from the Greeks to Freud*, Cambridge, MA: Harvard University Press, 1990.

Lenz, Carolyn; Swift, Ruth; Greene, Gayle; Neely, Carol Thomas (eds.), *The Woman's Part: Feminist Criticism of Shakespeare*, Urbana, Ill.: Illinois University Press, 1980.

Lévesque, Claude, *L'étrangeté du texte: Essais sur Nietzsche, Freud, Blanchot et Derrida*, Mintreal:VLB Editeur, 1976.

Linklater, Kristin, *Freeing the Natural Voice*, New York: Drama Book Specialists, 1976.

Llewelyn, John, *Derrida On the Threshold of Sense*, London: Macmillan, 1986.

Loomba, Ania, Orkin, Martin (eds.), *Post-Colonial Shakespeare*, London/New York: Routledge, 1998.

Lukacher, Ned, *Primal Scenes: Literature, Philosophy, Psychoanalysis*, Ithaca, N.Y.: Cornell University Press, 1986.

MacCary, W. Thomas, *Friends and Lovers: The Phenomenology of Desire in Shakespearean Comedy*, New York: Columbia University Press, 1985.

Marcus, L., *Puzzling Shakespeare: Local Reading and its Discontents*, Berkeley: California University Press, 1988.

Margolies, David, *Monsters of the Deep: Social Dissolution in Shakespeare's Tragedies*, Manchester: Manchester University Press, 1992.

Marshall, Cynthia, *Last Things and Last Plays: Shakespearean Eschatology*, Carbondale: Southern Illinois University Press, 1991.

Mayoux, Jean-Jacques, *Shakespeare*, Paris: Aubier Montaigne, 1983.

McElroy, B., *Shakespeare's Mature Tragedies*, New Jersey: Princeton University Press, 1973.

McLuhan, Marshall, *The Gutenberg Galaxy: The Making of Typographic Man*, London: Routledge, 1962.

Megill, Allan, *Prophets of Extremity: Nietzsche, Heidegger, Foucault, Derrida*, Berkeley: University of California Press, 1985.

Melchiori, Giorgio, *Shakespeare's Dramatic Meditations*, Oxford: Clarendon Press, 1976.

Merleau-Ponty, Maurice, *Signs,* trans. Richard C. McCleary, Evanson: Northwestern University Press, 1964.

—, *The Visible and the Invisible,* trans. Alphonso Lingis, Eavanson: Northwestern University Press, 1968.

Minazzoli, A., *La première ombre*, Paris: Minuit, 1990.

Mitchell, Juliet, "From King Lear to Anna 'O' and Beyond: Some Speculative Theses on Hysteria and the Traditionless Self," *Yale Journal of Criticism* 5:2, 1992.

Montaigne, Michel Eyquem (de), *Essais*, trans. in modern French by André Lanly, Paris: Editions Champion, 1989.

Motion, Andrew, *Keats*, London: Faber & Faber, 1997.

Muir, Kenneth and Schoenbaum, S., *A New Companion of Shakespeare's Studies,* London: Cambridge University Press, 1974.

Nietzsche, Friedrich, *The Gay Science*, trans. Walter Kaufmann, New York: Vintage Books, 1974.

—, *The Will To Power*, trans and ed. Walter Kaufmann, New York: Vintage Books, 1968.

Novy, Marianne, *Love's Argument: Gender Relations in Shakespeare*, Chapel Hill, NC: University of North Carolina Press, 1984.

Nuttall, A.D., *A New Mimesis: Shakespeare and the Representation of Reality*, London: Methuen, 1983.

Ondek Laurence, Patricia, *The Reading of Silence: Virginia Woolf in the English Tradition*, Stanford, CA: Stanford University Press, 1991.

Parker, Patricia, and Hartman, Geoffrey (eds.), *Shakespeare and the Question of Theory*, London & New York: Methuen, 1985.

Patterson, Annabel, *Shakespeare and the Popular Voice*, Oxford: Blackwell, 1989.

Pavis, Patrice, *Theatre at the Crossroads of Culture*, trans. Loren Kruger, London: Routledge, 1992.

Pechter, Edward (ed.), *Textual and Theatrical Shakespeare: Questions of Evidence*, Iowa City: University of Iowa Press, 1996.

Plato, *Symposium*, trans. Alexander Nehamas and Paul Woodruff, Indianapolis: Hackett Publishing, 1989.

Rabinow, Paul (ed.), *The Foucault Reader*, New York: Pantheon, 1984.

Rapaport, Herman, *Heidegger and Derrida. Reflections on Time and Language*, Lincoln and London: University of Nebraska, 1989.

Ricoeur, Paul, *Soi-même comme l'autre*, Paris: Seuil, 1990.

Rodenburg, Patsy, *The Need for Words: Voice and the Text*, New York: Routledge, 1993.

Rorty, Richard, *Philosophy and the Mirror of Nature*, Oxford: Blackwell, 1980.

Rosenberg, Marvin, *The Masks of King Lear*, Berkeley: University of California Press, 1972.

Rousseau, Jean-Jacques, *On the Origin of Language,* New York: F. Ungar, 1967.

Royle, Nicholas, *Telepathy and Literature: Essays on the Reading Mind*, Oxford, Cambridge, MA: Basil Blackwell, 1991.

Ryan, Kiernan, (ed.), *King Lear*, London: Macmillan, 1993.

—, *Shakespeare*, Brighton: Harvester, 1989.

Said, Edward W., *Culture & Imperialism,* New York: Columbia University Press, 1993.

—, *The World, the Text and the Critic*, Cambridge, MA: Harvard University Press, 1983.

Salkeld, Duncan, *Madness and Drama in the Age of Shakespeare*, Manchester: Manchester University Press, 1993.

Sallis, John, *Being and Logos: The Way of the Platonic Dialogue*, Atlantic Highlands: Humanities Press, 1898.

Scarry, Elaine, *The Body in Pain: The Making and Unmaking of the World*, New York: Oxford University Press, 1985.

Schiesari, Juliana, *The Gendering of Melancholia: Feminism, Psychoanalysis, and the Symbolics of Loss in Renaissance Literature,* Ithaca, N.Y.: Cornell University Press, 1992.

Schoenfeldt, Michael C., *Bodies and Selves in Early Modern England. Physiology and Inwardness in Spenser, Shakespeare, Herbert, and Milton*, Cambrige: Cambridge University Press, 1999.

Scholes, Robert, *Textual Power,* New Haven & London: Yale University Press, 1985.

Schrift, Alan D., *Nietzsche and the Question of Interpretation*, New York/London: Routledge, 1990.

Schulte, Anne-Lise, *Maurice Blanchot. L'écriture comme expérience du dehors*, Paris: Droz, 1983.

Schutte, Ofelia, *Beyond Nihilism: Nietzsche Without Masks,* Chicago: University of Chicago Press, 1984.

Searle, J., *Expression and Meaning*, Cambridge: Cambridge University Press, 1985.

Shapiro, James, *Shakespeare and the Jews*, New York: Columbia University Press, 1996.

Silverman, Hugh J., *Between Hermeneutics. Textualities and Deconstruction*, New York & London: Routledge, 1994.

Sinfield, Alan, *Faultlines: Cultural Materialism and the Politics of Dissident Reading*, Berkeley: University of California Press, 1992.

Skura, Meredith, *Shakespeare the Actor and the Purposes of Playing,* Chicago: University of Chicago Press, 1993.

Smith, Bruce R., *Homosexual Desire in Shakespeare's England: A Cultural Poetics*, Chicago: University of Chicago Press, 1991.

Smith, Paul, *Discerning the Subject*, Minneapolis: University of Minnesota Press, 1988.

Spurgeon, Caroline, *Shakespeare's Imagery and What it Tells us*, London: Cambridge University Press, 1935.

Starobinski, Jean, *The Living Eye*, trans. Arthur Goldhammer, Cambridge, MA, and London: Harvard University Press, 1989.

States, Bert O., *The Pleasure of the Play*, Ithaca, NY: Cornell University Press, 1994.

Steiner, George, *No Passion Spent. Essays 1978–1996*, London/Boston: Faber and Faber, 1996.

—, *Real Presences*, Chicago: The University of Chicago Press, 1991.

Strasberg, Lee, *A Dream of Passion: The Development of the Method* (ed.) Evangeline Morphos, Boston: Little/Brown, 1987.

Strawson, Peter F. (Sir), *Entity & Identity*, Oxford: Oxford University Press, 1997.

Taylor, Barry, *Vagrant Writing: Social and Semiotic Disorders in the English Renaissance*, Toronto: University of Toronto Press, 1991.

Taylor, Gary, *A Moment by Moment by Shakespeare*, London: Macmillan, 1985.

—, *Reinventing Shakespeare*, London: Hogarth Press, 1989.

Taylor, Mark C., *Imagologies. Media Philosophy*, New York: Routledge, 1994.

Tennenhouse, Leonard, *Power on Display: The Politics of Shakespeare's Genres*, London: Routledge, 1986.

Thom, Gary B., *The Human Nature of Social Discontent: Alienation, Anomie, Ambivalence*, Totowa, N.J.: Rowman and Allanheld, 1985.

Thompson, Ann, *King Lear: The Critics Debate*, London: Macmillan, 1988.

Thoreau, Henry D., "A Week on the Concord and Merrimac Rivers," in *The Writings of H. D. Thoreau*, ed. Carl F. Hovde & William L., Howarth, New Jersey: Princeton University Press, 1980.

Traub, Valerie, *Desire and Anxiety: Circulations of Sexuality in Shakespearean Drama*, London: Routledge, 1992.

Valéry, Paul, *Cahiers,* Paris: Bibliothèque de la Pléiade, Gallimard, 1974.

Vasse, Denis, *Le poids du réel, la souffrance,* Paris: Seuil, 1983.

—, *Le temps du désir. Essai sur le corps et la parole*, Paris: Seuil, 1997.

—, *Se tenir debout et marcher: du jardin oedipien à la vie en société*, Paris: Gallimard, 1995.

Vattimo, Gianni, *Oltre l'interpretazione,* Bari: Edizioni Laterza, 1994.

Veeser, H. Aram (ed.), *The New Historicism Reader*, London: Routledge, 1994.

Watson, Robert, *Shakespeare and the Hazards of Ambition*, Cambridge, MA: Harvard University Press, 1984.

—, *The Rest is Silence: Death as Annihilation in the English Renaissance*, Berkeley: University of California Press, 1994.

Weigel, Sigrid, *Body-and Image-Space. Re-reading Walter Benjamain*, London/New York: Routledge, 1996.

Weitz, Morris, *Hamlet and the Philosophy of Literary Criticism,* London: Faber & Faber, 1972.

White, Hayden, *The Content of the Form: Narrative and Historical Representation*, Baltimore/London: Johns Hopkins University Press, 1987.

White, Stephen, *Political Theory and Postmodernism*, Cambridge: Cambridge University Press, 1991.

Willbern, David, *Poetic Will. Shakespeare and the Play of Language*, Philadelphia: University of Pennsylvania Press, 1997.

Williams, Carlos William, *The Collected Poems,* New York: A New Directions Book, 1986.

Williams, Linda, *Hard Core: Power, Pleasure, and the "Frenzy of the Visible"*, Berkeley and Los Angeles: University of California Press, 1989.

Wilson, Richard, *Will Power. Essays on Shakespearean Authority*, New York, London, Toronto: Harvester/Wheatsheaf, 1993.

Winnicott, D.W., *Playing and Reality*, London: Tavistock, 1970.

Wood, David, *Deconstruction of Time*, Atlantic Highlands, New Jersey: Humanities Press, 1988.

Woolf, Virginia, *A Room of One's Own,* London: Penguin, 1945.

—, *The Waves*, Middlesex: Penguin Books Ltd, Harmondsworth, 1974.

Worthen, W.B., *Shakespeare and the Authority of Performance*, Cambridge: Cambridge University Press, 1997.

Yates, Frances A., *The Art of Memory*, London: Routledge/Kegan Paul, 1966.

Zarrilli, Philip B. (ed.), *Acting (Re)Considered: Theories and Practices*, London: Routledge, 1995.

Zizek, Slavoj, *For They Know Not What They Do: Enjoyment as a Political Factor*, London: Verso, 1991.

INDEX

FORECAAST

(Forum for European Contributions to African American Studies)

Dorothea Fischer-Hornung; Alison D. Goeller (eds.)
EmBODYing Liberation
The Black Body in American Dance
A collection of essays concerning the black body in American dance, *EmBODYing Liberation* serves as an important contribution to the growing field of scholarship in African American dance, in particular the strategies used by individual artists to contest and liberate racialized stagings of the black body. The collection features special essays by Thomas DeFrantz and Brenda Dixon Gottschild, as well as an interview with Isaac Julien.
Bd. 4, 2001, 152 S., 20,90 €, br., ISBN 3-8258-4473-0

Patrick B. Miller; Therese Frey Steffen; Elisabeth Schäfer-Wünsche (eds.)
The Civil Rights Movement Revisited
Critical Perspectives on the Struggle for Racial Equality in the United States
The crusade for civil rights was a defining episode of 20th century U.S. history, reshaping the constitutional, political, social, and economic life of the nation. This collection of original essays by both European and American scholars includes close analyses of literature and film, historical studies of significant themes and events from the turn-of-the century to the movement years, and assessments of the movement's legacies. Ultimately, the articles help examine the ways civil rights activism, often grounded in the political work of women, has shaped American consciousness and culture until the outset of the 21st century.
Bd. 5, 2001, 224 S., 24,90 €, br., ISBN 3-8258-4486-2

Fritz Gysin; Christopher Mulvey (Eds.)
Black Liberation in the Americas
The recognition that Africans in the Americas have also been subjects of their destiny rather than merely passive objects of European oppression represents one of the major shifts in twentieth-century mainstream historiography. Yet even in the eighteenth and nineteenth centuries, slave narratives and abolitionist tracts offered testimony to various ways in which Africans struggled against slavery, from outright revolt to day-to-day resistance. In the first decades of the twentieth century, African American historians like Carter G. Woodson and W. E. B. Du Bois started to articulate a vision of African American history that emphasized survival and resistance rather than victimization and oppression. This volume seeks to address these and other issues in black liberation from interdisciplinary and comparative perspectives, focusing on such issues as slave revolts, day-to-day resistance, abolitionist movements, maroon societies, the historiography of resistance, the literature of resistance, black liberation movements in the twentieth century, and black liberation and post colonial theory. The chapters span the disciplines of history, literature, anthropology, folklore, film, music, architecture, and art, drawing on the black experience of liberation in the United States, the Caribbean, and Latin America.
Bd. 6, 2001, 280 S., 24,90 €, br., ISBN 3-8258-5137-0

Justine Tally
The Story of *Jazz*
Toni Morrison's Dialogic Imagination
Ever since its publication in 1992, *Jazz*, probably Toni Morrison's most difficult novel to date, has elicited a wide array of critical response. Many of these analyses, while both thoughtful and thought-provoking, have provided only partial or inherently inconclusive interpretations. The title, and certain of the author's own pronouncements, have led other critics to focus on the music itself, both as medium and aesthetic support for the narration.
Bd. 7, 2001, 168 S., 20,90 €, br., ISBN 3-8258-5364-0

Mar Gallego
Passing Novels in the Harlem Renaissance
Identity Politics and Textual Strategies
Passing Novels in the Harlem Renaissance offers an insightful study of the significance of passing novels for the literary and intellectual debate of the Harlem Renaissance. Mar Gallego effectively uncovers the presence of a subversive component in five of these novels (by James Weldon Johnson, George Schuyler, Nella Larsen, and Jessie Fauset), turning them into useful tools to explore the passing phenomenon in all its richness and complexity. Her compelling study intends to contribute to the ongoing revision of the parameters conventionally employed to analyze passing novels by drawing attention to a great variety of textual strategies such as double consciousness, parody, and multiple generic covers. Examining the hybrid nature of these texts, Gallego skillfully highlights their radical critique of the status quo and their celebration of a distinct African American identity.
"*Passing Novels in the Harlem Renaissance* is an impressive work of scholarship and interpretation. It is well researched and stimulating to read."
Hanna Wallinger, University of Salzburg
"Mar Gallego draws our renewed attention to the uses and subversions of the trope of passing that have characterized the African American

LIT Verlag Münster – Hamburg – Berlin – London
Grevener Str./Fresnostr. 2 48159 Münster
Tel.: 0251 – 23 50 91 – Fax: 0251 – 23 19 72
e-Mail: vertrieb@lit-verlag.de – http://www.lit-verlag.de

novelistic tradition also in the twentieth century." Giulia Fabi, University of Ferrara "Mar Gallego's thorough scholarship now provides us with a new, in-depth and refreshing reading of texts we thought we already knew something about. A provocative text and a welcome addition to the field!" Justine Tally, University of La Laguna
Bd. 8, 2003, 224 S., 24,90 €, br., ISBN 3-8258-5842-1

Paola Boi; Sabine Broeck (Eds.)
CrossRoutes – The Meanings of "Race" for the 21st Century
This collection reflects the still urgent project of historical recuperation, as well as an examination of literary representations and other cultural manifestations of the Black Diaspora. Disciplinary work within the boundaries of African American Studies has been enhanced by more general considerations of the history of rr-aceänd racism in globalized contexts. The articles assembled here reflect recent empirical research as well as challenging theoretical considerations. Contributions address particular formations of racialized modernity owed to the impact of the Atlantic slave trade and slavery, and thus broaden the approach to the Middle Passage, to improve our understanding of it as a constitutive transatlantic phenomenon in the widest possible sense.
Bd. 9, 2003, 272 S., 25,90 €, br., ISBN 3-8258-6651-3

Sylvia Mayer (ed.)
Restoring the Connection to the Natural World
Essays on the African American Environmental Imagination
Since its emergence in the second half of the nineteenth century American environmentalism had predominantly been a white, middle-class pursuit, preoccupied with notions of wilderness and wildlife preservation. Only fairly recently, with the advent of the environmental justice movement in the 1980s, has American environmentalism broadened its definition of "environment" to include the concerns relevant to a community's way of living. Especially the concerns of poor urban communities of color, which have been exposed to environmental hazards disproportionately, have entered the political agenda. This volume - one of the first collections of ecocritical essays devoted exclusively to African American texts - shows that African Americans have contributed to the efforts of the environmental justice movement not only as political activists, but also as writers. The essays range from studies of nineteenth-century slave narratives to twentieth-century texts

by Zora Neale Hurston, Claude McKay, Richard Wright, Charles Johnson, Toni Cade Bambara, Audre Lorde, and Octavia Butler. Employing a variety of theoretical and methodological premises, they provide insight into the texts' various conceptualizations of "nature," "culture," and "humanness" and their implications for environmental ethics.
Bd. 10, 2003, 208 S., 20,90 €, br., ISBN 3-8258-6732-3

Kimberley Phillips; Hermine Pinson; Lorenzo Thomas; Hanna Wallinger (eds.)
Critical Voicings of Black Liberation
Resistance and Representations in the Americas
The contributions to "Critical Voices of Black Liberation in the Americas" originated from the 1999 CAAR Conference in Münster and from conferences held in the US in 2000 and 2001. More than half of the eleven essays consider black performances on stage, in sound, and on film; the remaining essays explore slavery, African American literature, and nineteenth-century black educators. These exciting essays creatively examine artistic and/or political articulation of black liberation as the construction of a new critical and signifyin(g) voice. This liberated and critical voice asserts itself as much as a communal expression of black subjectivities as it is an articulation of the black self.
Bd. 11, 2003, 192 S., 20,90 €, br., ISBN 3-8258-6739-0

Ana María Manzanas; Jesús Benito
Intercultural Mediations
Hybridity and Mimesis in American Literatures
Intercultural Mediations proposes a study of the multiple crossings between and among the different literary traditions of the United States. The volume draws upon two main theoretical sources, namely postcolonial theory and American Border Studies, and aims to articulate a model of the hybrid, postcolonial and liminal nature of writing in the US. Ana Mª Manzanas and Jesús Benito explore the nature of the ëthnicÖthers' appropriation, dialogization and Subversion of the Euroamerican authoritative discourse – embodied in what the authors call the Book of the West – as well as the inscription of cultural difference on the white page. Their analysis focuses on the production of contestatory sites of enunciation in a few particular fields and texts from the literatures of the US, such as John Milton Oskison's The Problem of Old Harjo,Toni Morrison's Beloved, Helena Viramontes's The Cariboo Café,Carlos Fuentes's La frontera de crystal, Ron Arias's The Road to Tamazunchale, Frederick Douglass's Narrative, Louise Erdrich's Tracks, José Barreiro's

LIT Verlag Münster – Hamburg – Berlin – London
Grevener Str./Fresnostr. 2 48159 Münster
Tel.: 0251 – 23 50 91 – Fax: 0251 – 23 19 72
e-Mail: vertrieb@lit-verlag.de – http://www.lit-verlag.de

The Indian Chronicles, and Caryl Phillip's Crossing the River. The authors use a comparative approach which underscores the aesthetic and epistemic ruptures that ethnic and marginalized wridng is producing on Westem culture's general text, in order to open up new sites of enunciation and new spaces for the hybridizaäon of traditional hegemonic discourses.

Bd. 12, 2003, 224 S., 25,90 €, br., ISBN 3-8258-6738-2

Studien zur englischen Literatur
herausgegeben von Prof. Dr. Dieter Mehl
(Universität Bonn)

Ulrike Horstmann
Die Namen in Edmund Spensers Versepos
The Faerie Queene: *Immortal Name*,
Memorable Name, *Well-becoming Name*
Zu den auffälligen Merkmalen von Edmund Spensers Versepos *The Faerie Queene* gehören die offensichtlich bedeutungsvollen Namen. Viele von ihnen sind leicht zu entschlüsseln, aber damit beginnt ihre Faszination erst. Die Namen erfüllen die unterschiedlichsten Funktionen im Text: Sie tragen bei zur Charakterisierung von Figuren und Orten und untermalen die Atmosphäre von Situationen. Sie verbinden und kontrastieren Figuren und bauen Spannungsfelder zwischen der Bedeutung eines Namens und den Namenträgern auf. Spenser folgt nicht dogmatisch einem philosophischen Konzept der Bedeutung von Namen, sondern setzt die Namen je nach Bedarf ein, sowohl für allegorische Sinngebung als auch zur Schaffung von Komik.
Aufbauend auf einer neu entwickelten Typologie der Bedeutungskonstitution durch Namen in literarischen Texten, konzentriert sich die vorliegende Untersuchung der Namen in *The Faerie Queene* dementsprechend weniger auf die etymologische Bedeutung von Namen als vielmehr auf das Wechselspiel von Namen und Bedeutungen im Text. So kann anhand von Hauptfiguren wie dem Redcrosse Knight, Una und Guyon gezeigt werden, daß die Deutung der Namen neue und fesselnde Ansätze zur Interpretation bietet.

Bd. 10, 2001, 320 S., 25,90 €, br., ISBN 3-8258-4872-8

Christa Jansohn
Zweifelhafter Shakespeare
Zu den Shakespeare-Apokryphen und ihrer Rezeption von der Renaissance bis zum 20. Jahrhundert
Die Arbeit gibt einen historischen Überblick über die Geschichte der Shakespeare-Apokryphen, analysiert die Problematik apokrypher Dramen und stellt am Beispiel von *Arden of Faversham*

exemplarisch die Rezeptionsgeschichte von der Renaissance bis zum 20. Jahrhundert in England, Amerika und Deutschland dar. Zudem wird die nur in einem Manuskript überlieferte und äußerst schwer zugängliche Verarbeitung von Jacob Geis' Bühnenbearbeitung des Dramas *(Elisabethanische Tragödie, Arden von Feversham, 1931)* kritisch ediert.

Bd. 11, 2000, 448 S., 35,90 €, gb., ISBN 3-8258-5133-8

Axel Stähler
"Perpetuall Monuments"
Die Repräsentation von Architektur in der italienischen Festdokumentation
(ca. 1515 – 1640) und der englischen *court masque* (1604 – 1640)
In den (höfischen) Festen der Renaissance und des frühen Barock kam der Architektur – etwa von Triumphbögen und Saaleinrichtungen oder Proszeniumsbögen, aber auch der in Bühnenbildern dargestellten Architektur – eminente Bedeutung zu: bei der Definition des festlichen Repräsentationsraumes und als Bedeutungsträger. Diese interdisziplinär angelegte Studie konzentriert sich in einer komparatistischen Untersuchung auf die Repräsentation von Architektur in den gedruckten Beschreibungen italienischer Feste zwischen 1515 und 1640 und in den publizierten Texten der englischen *court masque* der frühen Stuartzeit (1603 – 49), in denen sowohl das italienische Festwesen als auch die italienische Festdokumentation als immer wieder anzitiertes Referenzsystem stets präsent war. Ihr Erkenntnisinteresse ist weniger auf das Repräsentierte gerichtet als auf den Repräsentationsmodus, es zielt demgemäß nicht primär auf die Rekonstruktion der dokumentierten Festarchitektur, sondern gilt vor allem der Festdokumentation selbst, die also nicht so sehr in ihrer Wirklichkeitabbildenden als vielmehr in ihrer wirklichkeitbildenden Funktion in den Blick genommen wird, als eigene Gattung mit distinktiven Merkmalen, mit eigenständiger literarischer, kunstliterarischer und ästhetischer Qualität.

Bd. 12, 2001, 584 S., 35,90 €, gb., ISBN 3-8258-5142-7

Anne-Julia Zwierlein
Majestick Milton
British Imperial Expansion and Transformations of *Paradise Lost*, 1667 – 1837
This study investigates how Milton's texts, above all *Paradise Lost*, were read in the context of eighteenth- and early-nineteenth-century British empire building. Milton's epic was implicated in the articulation and criticism of early modem colonialist discourse; it also lent itself easily to later imperial and anti-imperial appropriations. Milton the 'national

LIT Verlag Münster – Hamburg – Berlin – London
Grevener Str./Fresnostr. 2 48159 Münster
Tel.: 0251 – 23 50 91 – Fax: 0251 – 23 19 72
e-Mail: vertrieb@lit-verlag.de – http://www.lit-verlag.de

poet' emerged from the strife between Whigs and Tories for his legacy; this book analyses Milton's presence in a number of discourses that are characteristic of the Whig model of secular history: the discourses about empire, language and literary criticism, travelling and astronomy, agriculture, commerce and *Pax Britannica,* as well as the slave-trade. The temporal frame extends from the Restoration through the loss of the American colonies to the Second British Empire and 'Milton in India'. Eighteenth-century British national epics, commented Milton editions and poetic Milton recreations invented a tradition for the British Empire and reintroduced the Virgilian concept of *translatio imperii,* transforming Milton's allegories of divine power into descriptions of secular authority. This study contextualizes traditional stories about 'Milton and Romanticism' by examining mostly 'minor' writers; still, Dryden, Johnson, Pope and Blake feature in some detail. The epilogue shows that even postcolonial rewritings of Milton make more sense in the light of the eighteenth-century Milton and his presence in the nineteenth-century British colonial education syllabus.
Bd. 13, 2001, 512 S., 65,90 €, gb., ISBN 3-8258-5432-9

Astrid Laupichler
Lachen und Weinen: tragikomisch-karnevaleske Entwicklungsräume
Interpretationen zu Shakespeares Problemstücken und Romanzen
Bd. 14, 2002, 432 S., 35,90 €, gb., ISBN 3-8258-5824-3

Christa Jansohn (Hg.)
In the Footsteps of Queen Victoria: Wege zum Viktorianischen Zeitalter
Das viktorianische Zeitalter gehört zweifellos zu den interessantesten und gleichzeitig vielschichtigsten Gebieten der englischen Literatur. Der Band versammelt 16 Beiträge, die anläßlich des hundertsten Todesjahres der Königin Victoria im Rahmen einer Ringvorlesung am Centre for British Studies in Bamberg gehalten wurden. Die in deutscher und englischer Sprache verfaßten Beiträge renommierter Forscher und Forscherinnen sollen einen Einblick in die verschiedenen Gebiete des viktorianischen Zeitalters geben. Der Band ist in folgende Abschnitte unterteilt: 1. Cultural Memories, or Images of Queen Victoria, 2. Science, Society and Victorian Culture, und 3. Reading and Writing in Victorian England. Eine ausführliche Bibliographie rundet den Band ab und soll zur weiteren Beschäftigung mit dem viktorianischen Zeitalter anregen.
Bd. 15, 2003, 352 S., 25,90 €, br., ISBN 3-8258-5884-7

André Schüller
A Life Composed
T. S. Eliot and the Morals of Modernism
Bd. 17, 2002, 368 S., 24,90 €, br., ISBN 3-8258-6362-x

Anglistik / Amerikanistik

Jörg Rademacher (Hrsg./Ed.)
Modernism and the Individual Talent/Moderne und besondere Begabung
Re-Canonizing Ford Madox Ford (Hueffer)/Zur Re-Kanonisierung von Ford Madox Ford (Hüffer). Symposium Münster June/Juni 1999
Bd. 6, 2002, 224 S., 25,90 €, br., ISBN 3-8258-4311-4

Ulrike Ernst
From Anti-Apartheid to African Renaissance
Interviews with South African Writers and Critics on Cultural Politics Beyond the Cultural Struggle
Bd. 7, 2002, 208 S., 20,90 €, br., ISBN 3-8258-5804-9

Andreas Lienkamp; Wolfgang Werth; Christian Berkemeier (Hg.)
"As strange as the world"
Annäherungen an das Werk des Erzählers und Filmemachers Paul Auster
Bd. 8, 2002, 170 S., 20,90 €, br., ISBN 3-8258-6046-9

Victor Grove
Hamlet
Das Drama des modernen Menschen
Bd. 10, 2003, 248 S., 30,90 €, br., ISBN 3-8258-6224-0

Hans Werner Breunig
Verstand und Einbildungskraft in der englischen Romantik
S. T. Coleridge als Kulminationspunkt seiner Zeit
Bd. 11, 2003, 352 S., 25,90 €, br., ISBN 3-8258-6244-5

Birgit Lahaye
Pirating History
Die Darstellung des haitianischen Unabhängigkeitskampfes in der Erzählliteratur
Bd. 12, 2003, 288 S., 29,90 €, br., ISBN 3-8258-6718-8

LIT Verlag Münster – Hamburg – Berlin – London
Grevener Str./Fresnostr. 2 48159 Münster
Tel.: 0251 – 23 50 91 – Fax: 0251 – 23 19 72
e-Mail: vertrieb@lit-verlag.de – http://www.lit-verlag.de